100% REAL

NO ARTIFICIAL COLORS OR FLAVORS

100% REAL

100 INSANELY GOOD RECIPES
FOR CLEAN FOOD MADE FRESH

SAM TALBOT

Oxmoor
House.

© 2016 Time Inc. Books
Lifestyle photography © 2016 Evan Sung

Published by Oxmoor House, an imprint of
Time Inc. Books
225 Liberty Street, New York, NY 10281

Writer: Susanna Margolis
Senior Editor: Betty Wong
Project Editor: Melissa Brown
Designer: Allison Chi
Photographers: Iain Bagwell, Caitlin Bensel,
    Jennifer Causey, Greg Dupree, Victor Protasio,
    Hector Sanchez, Evan Sung
Prop Stylists: Jessie Baude, Kay E. Clarke,
    Missie Crawford, Andrea Greco, Morgan Locke
Food Stylists: Kellie Kelley, Maria del Mar, Margaret
    Monroe Dickey, Blakeslee Giles, Rishon Hanners,
    Will Smith
Illustrator: Debbie Fong
Recipe Developers and Testers: Jiselle Basile,
    Nathan Carrabba, Torie Cox, Mark Driskill,
    Emily Hall, Julia Levy, Pam Lolley, Robby Melvin,
    Callie Nash, Karen Rankin, Amanda Williams,
    Marianne Williams, Deb Wise
Assistant Production Director: Sue Chodakiewicz
Assistant Production Manager: Diane Rose Keener
Copy Editors: Rebecca Brennan, Dolores Hydock
Proofreader: Adrienne Davis
Indexer: Mary Ann Laurens
Fellows: Helena Joseph, Hailey Middlebrook,
    Kyle Grace Mills

ISBN-13: 978-0-8487-4676-6
Library of Congress Control Number: 2016950230

First Edition 2016

Printed in China

10 9 8 7 6 5 4 3 2 1

We welcome your comments and suggestions about
Time Inc. Books.
Please write to us at:
Time Inc. Books
Attention: Book Editors
P.O. Box 62310
Tampa, Florida 33662-2310

Time Inc. Books products may be purchased for business
or promotional use. For information on bulk purchases,
please contact Christi Crowley in the Special Sales
Department at (845) 895-9858.

For the ones who remain different, stay messy, keep your hearts hungry and your souls thirsty. Don't lose the weird; it's why we love you. Do it your way because nobody else can.

For my mom, Diane, the sweetest, most compassionate, bravest, badass woman I know

For Joel, my manager, my dearest friend, my calendar, and my consigliere

CONTENTS

INTRODUCTION

I suppose it's because I'm both a chef and a type 1 diabetic that I'm forever being asked questions about what I eat. People want to know which diet I follow: Paleo? Vegetarian? Vegan? "What foods are you allowed to eat?" they ask me. "What foods are absolutely forbidden? Are you gluten-free? Dairy-free? Sugar-free? Fun-free? Taste-free?"

The simple answer to all these questions is: none of the above. What I eat, simply put, is 100% real food. While I've learned things from all of the eating styles I'm asked about, and while following a specific diet for a month or more at various times in my life has taught me a lot about what I can eat to still feel well and balanced, I have chosen a much simpler philosophy—to eat real food.

That's the philosophy. In practice, sure, some of the real food I eat is gluten-free. Almost all of it is dairy-free and sugar-free. Some of what I eat may look like the Paleo diet, while a great deal of what I eat—most of what I eat, in fact—is plant based: a whole lot of vegetables and fruits. But the bottom line is still that fundamentally simple guideline: at mealtime or snack time, in a restaurant or at home, for a fancy banquet or for something I just slap together when I get in the mood, I eat real food. It gives me more energy, lets me control my weight, keeps my mood high, and enables me to stay in tune with the day-to-day grind.

Just what I mean by real food, why it's the basis of lifetime health, and how it opens a world of lip-smacking meal experiences to last a lifetime—a healthy, fulfilling lifetime—is what this book is all about.

Sure, I'm talking about food that is as whole and as natural as it can be and that you get as fresh and locally as possible—as close to its source and as close to nature as can be managed. As a chef, I am here to tell you that striving for "local" and "natural" does not mean limiting yourself in any way. Real food represents the greatest variety of tastes, textures, and flavors of any "diet" plan and offers the most possibilities for creativity in the kitchen. This book will show you that in a hundred different ways—100 recipes for 100 different meals, snacks, and special occasions.

I've been putting these recipes together for some time, because since I was a kid, eating real food has been absolutely natural to me. I still remember my first taste of farm-fresh eggs and just-picked vegetables. I was visiting my grandparents in rural Ohio, and the eggs and veggies came from a neighbor's farm. Wow. Tasting them was an eye-opener. Meanwhile, back home on the South Carolina coast, I learned to use a fishing rod about the same time I learned to draw with crayons, and the snapper, bass, and blue crab I brought home for my mother to prepare were barely out of the water when we sat down to eat them. Straight off the farm and right out of the water, this was real food, tastier and more satisfying to me by far than the trans-fatty snacks or sugar-laden cereals or prepackaged meals I really couldn't eat as I grew older because of my diabetes. Freshness became a kind of gold standard I would seek out for the rest of my life; I wanted everything I consumed to have that same taste of genuineness.

By the time I was in high school, I had my first cooking job, and as cooking became my passion, it also became my vocation. Now that I've been at it for a while, I can confirm that the closer our eating can stay to nature, the better off we are in terms of health and the more delicious our meals will be. Mama Nature has simply given us something that is divine; the more we can rely on her gifts, the better off we'll be. Nature won't let you down.

But of course, no food can really be forbidden. Trying to outlaw even a single fruit didn't work in the Garden of Eden, and it won't work today. Besides, eating shouldn't be restrictive, nerve-racking, or crazy complicated. It's eating, after all—something we all have to do pretty much every day. No point getting nutty about it. Fortunately, however, eating can and should be one of the great joys of life—and, as you'll see in the pages that follow, a creative adventure as well.

They say that if nondiabetics ate the way we diabetics have to eat, they'd be the healthiest people on earth, and the rates of obesity, heart disease, and other debilitating ailments would plummet. What I know for sure is this: there is nothing better for us and nothing that tastes better than 100% real food.

HONEY

Sometimes the name
apples are honey sw
crisp, some say "exp
new variety continu
introduction in Minn
more Honeysnap tre

What's It Like?

Best Uses

Special Hint

Availability

WHAT'S REAL AND WHAT'S NOT?

What do I mean by 100% real food?

Mussels just off the boat certainly qualify. So do tomatoes somebody pulled off the vine an hour ago. Fruits and vegetables in season, fresh as they can be . . . eggs from the farm . . . a many-colored salad with pea shoots and raspberries picked just this morning . . . or a honey crunch granola with blueberries, coconut, and lime that you made yourself: they all constitute 100% real food.

But so does pizza. It was invented by peasants in southern Italy who couldn't afford to throw out their homemade bread even after it got stale. So they hacked off a slice, went out into the garden and grabbed a tomato off the vine, layered on a hunk of cheese they made from water buffalo milk, drizzled olive oil over it, and stuffed the whole thing into the oven. What a concept—all sorts of real foods put together—and what a fantastic result.

You can say the same for a Dark Chocolate Soufflé with Rum Cream and a coconut caramel sauce (page 220). Or for a Warm Bacon, Avocado and Comté sandwich (page 81) or Italian Shrimp and Grits (page 153). All 100% real—all pretty close to the way nature created them and tasting of it too.

What do I mean by foods that are not real? Certainly topping the list are the so-called fabricated foods—meat analogs, for example, or imitation dairy products. The U.S. Patent Office describes fabricated foods as "prepared by shaping a blend of edible textured protein particles, including single cell protein, bound together with a whey protein concentrate composition having more than 30% protein which is capable of forming a gel at 15% solids within 30 minutes when heated at 85°C." I don't know about you, but as meal descriptions go, that one is a major turnoff—something I really, really would not like to put into my mouth for any reason.

So Hamburger Helper does not make my personal list of real food. But if you crave the taste of hamburger and pasta, it is just as easy to get it from real food. Use some organic ground beef, mix it into just about any form of pasta, add a bit of cheese, and you have the taste you want but in a form that is even more delicious than the packaged kind—and is far better for your health.

100% HEALTHY?

Keep in mind, however, that while eating clean, real food pretty much all of the time doesn't mean restricting yourself to eating a garden salad every day of the week, it also doesn't mean eating hamburger and pasta every day either.

Instead, it's about striking a balance between the two—a place between relying exclusively on fresh vegetables in season and eating just meat and pasta. Neither extreme can keep you satisfied forever, and the meat and pasta version will eventually expand your waistline, burden your heart, and just might send you to an early grave. Instead, as much as possible, you want the place in between to be a place where you can be comfortable eating what you know is good for you and enjoying what you eat.

For example, the sinful chocolate soufflé with coconut caramel is food made with natural ingredients, and as an occasional indulgence, it is by no means equivalent to unhealthy eating, especially if balanced by a diet filled with the vegetables, good carbs, and lean proteins we all know we're supposed to eat. But no doctor is going to recommend it as a habitual dessert. That's where the balance tilts over into harmful.

Another example: both red meat and dairy products are real food. Does that mean it's healthy to eat a cheeseburger every day? I think we all know that it isn't. So while eating real food is a way to eat healthfully, it's still up to you to choose the way you balance your food options to achieve the highest level of healthful eating.

That means it's important to keep in mind, for example, that cheese, like all dairy, is not something to go overboard with. Sure, mother's milk is essential—for the earliest months of life especially. But dairy can be tough to digest and may raise cholesterol levels, two reasons that I tend to eat cheese rarely and in moderation. But cheese is also a universal favorite and a wonderful ingredient, so you will find it in a number of recipes in this book.

As for red meat, another animal product, I probably don't have to tell you about how its saturated fat content and LDL cholesterol can raise your risk of heart attack. My guess is that you've heard that lecture before.

Look, I know that cheese can be one of the superb tastes on the planet, and great cuisines like the French and Italian sing its praises and make liberal use of it. And I, too, love a great steak—once in a while. Later on in this book, I'll provide recipes that give you the same taste you love about red meat using substitute ingredients that save you the high cost to your health. You'll see how to substitute mushrooms to capture the taste of meat in lasagna. Or instead of cheese, try using almond cheese, avocado, or butternut squash, as much of an un-cheese as there is, to give some of the same creamy effect in a sandwich or your morning eggs. On the other hand, if cheese is something you love or red meat is something you crave, at least be aware when you choose to eat either or both—and right the balance at the next meal you eat. In other words, on those preferably rare occasions when only a cheeseburger will do, go for it, but at the next meal, make the healthier choice.

What's truly unhealthy, in my view, is making ourselves crazy over all this. The world of 100% real food is so wide and varied that the possibilities are endless—and endlessly inspiring. Emphasize the really good-for-us foods, scatter variety throughout your choices, and yield to the sinful indulgences when you get a craving you just can't escape. Do that and you can be 100% sure you and your family are eating healthfully and very, very well.

One additional note: the fact that I have included gluten- and dairy-free recipes in this book doesn't mean that I personally am gluten- and dairy-free. I'm not, but I focus on gluten- and dairy-free recipes because they often rely more heavily on fresh and clean produce, smart protein, and healthier fats. Also, I know that many people who follow my work and love my recipes adhere to diets that avoid gluten and/or dairy. They do so for health reasons or as a personal choice, and, obviously, I respect that. I've marked the recipes in this book that are vegetarian **V**, vegan **VG**, gluten-free **GF**, and dairy-free **DF** so you can easily identify them. I want this book to be a resource for those of you following a specific diet as well as for the folks looking specifically to eat more wholesome real food. So whatever category you belong to, this book is for you.

5 STEPS TO KEEPING IT REAL

Here's my quick, five-step guide to keeping it 100% real without getting crazy complicated or worrying you're losing out:

1 EAT PLANTS AND GREEN *FOR REAL*.

My goal each day is to eat as many vegetables and fruits as possible. At breakfast, lunch, dinner, and in snacks, I try to pack in as much produce as possible. The more vegetables and fruits I eat—fresh or frozen, green or blue, red or purple, yellow or orange—the better I feel. You will, too.

2 COOK AT HOME AT LEAST THREE TIMES A WEEK.

I'm a working dad of three dogs. The convenience of eating out or ordering easy takeout can be very tempting, especially at the end of an exhausting day. But no matter how tired I may feel, I try to eat the majority of meals at home—or I cook up homemade meals I can eat on the go. Cooking at home allows me to control the types of ingredients I use and their quality. It means I know what's in my meal, and just as important, I know what's not in my meal. The meals you cook at home don't have to be fancy, but when you're the captain and you've steered the operation, even a simple, 100% real meal you've created at home is better than eating out or ordering out—hands down.

3 DON'T EAT FABRICATED OR SUPER PROCESSED FOODS.

This one is huge, but let me be clear as to what we're talking about. Frozen foods and canned fish and even most condiments in jars are not part of this category. Yes, processing plants take a perishable fruit like fresh blueberries and immediately freeze them; in fact, they use a process called flash-freezing that subjects the berries to below-freezing temperatures right away. The nutritional result is as good as—some people say even better than—eating the berries in season right off the bush; all of the nutritional power of blueberries, which is substantial by the way, is preserved, and the taste is pretty authentic as well. As for canned fish, unless you live fairly near a body of water, you have little opportunity to enjoy fresh fish, so canned tuna or salmon or sardines preserve both the nutrition and the taste sensation that these foods contain. Just make sure the fish were caught smartly and sustainably—that is, keeping our oceans clean and our supply of fish and seafood abundant for generations to come.

So what I'm talking about when I say fabricated or highly processed foods are the boxes of breakfast cereals, the bottles and cans of "imitation" fruit juices or made-up sodas, the artificial "lunch meats" so filled with additives to extend shelf life and "create" flavor they have lost all relation to food at all. These highly processed foods contain masses of artificial ingredients, colors, and preservatives. Plus, when it comes to nutritional value, they're typically empty. I'll happily eat real cheese or pasta—just so long as I start off the next morning with an avocado smoothie—but you'll rarely find me eating a box of processed crackers or drinking a diet soda. It's just not worth the cost in how I look and feel.

If you're not sure whether a food is processed or not, follow the six-ingredient rule: If the label lists six ingredients or fewer, give the food a try to see if it's real. If there are more than six ingredients listed on the package, walk away—*unless* they are actual foods. For example, there's a fruit strip I love whose ingredients are apples, cherries, orange juice, orange pulp, and water; I'm cool with all of those ingredients. There are energy bars with a dozen ingredients, but they're all things like whole-grain oats, almonds, brown rice, cranberries, soybeans, flaxseed, and coconut. Can't argue with that.

But if the ingredients listed are unrecognizable or difficult to pronounce, they are almost certainly synthetic chemicals and chances are good the food is in no way real. A label listing like this—with disodium guanylate, FD&C Yellow Nos. 5 and 6, ascorbic acid, citric acid, sodium benzoate, calcium propionate, sodium erythorbate, calcium sorbate, potassium sorbate, and EDTA—doesn't sound too appetizing anyway, does it?

There's more!

FOCUS ON FFP—THE FAT, FIBER, AND PROTEIN SUPER TRIO.

I try to eat the trio—the whole combination—at every meal and at snacks. I suggest you do the same. Focus on the fat part especially. For me, that means eating healthy fat all day every day: avocados, nuts, olive oil, coconut anything, yogurt—even butter, Dude! But I laugh at—and totally avoid—anything labeled "low-fat" or "reduced-fat;" those are marketing slogans, and they're meaningless. When I focus on this super trio, I feel fuller, have more energy, and find it easier to maintain the mojo of my personal vibe.

FIND THE FUN IN FOOD; DON'T BE A JUDGMENTAL JERK

While I try to focus 100% on eating 100% real food, I refuse to get hung up on the need to achieve perfection. Perfection is like a unicorn: there's just no such thing. So if one day you indulge in pasta with butter, Parmesan cheese, and red chile flakes, then right on and good for you! I do it, too. If you let your kids eat a hamburger and fries off the kids' menu at your favorite restaurant, I'm right there with you. I think today's health and wellness experts put way too much pressure on all of us to be saints when it comes to eating, as if there

were some moral superiority involved in avoiding sugar. It comes off instead as being super restrictive (not to mention kind of obnoxious), and I, for one, am so not about that. Instead, I want you to find the joy in eating, whether you find it in nutrient-dense real food or otherwise. So if you need some ice cream once in a while, eat the freaking ice cream—with no shame. Just maybe reach for the coconut- or cashew-based dairy-free version of it (pages 212 and 215). And for your next meal or snack, come back to fresh, real food.

REAL FOOD KITCHEN

Step 1: Overhaul Your Pantry. Sometimes I peek into the pantries or refrigerators of friends or neighbors and wonder if a natural disaster is imminent. They're stocked for Armageddon, and the problem with that is that it really ups the ante on temptation. It also means you end up throwing a lot of stuff away; by the time you work your way to the back of the pantry, even the things with the longest shelf life have had it. So an overstuffed pantry or fridge can end up being wasteful—and very often costly.

The pantry shouldn't be either of those things. It is the place for basics, and the basics are pretty simple. The must-haves are oils, vinegars, dried herbs, alternatives to white flour if you're a baker, and various "elevators," as folks in the culinary world call them—namely, the spices and condiments and flavorings that appeal to your sense of taste and that enhance your enjoyment of food.

That really doesn't add up to a lot of items. And the first step toward making room for the must-haves is to get rid of the things that don't belong in your pantry at all.

ITEMS FOR THE SCRAP HEAP

You can make a fair amount of room in the cabinet or closet you use as your pantry by tossing out any sort of hydrogenated oil or trans-fatty food; in other words, toss out the canola oil, hydrogenated corn oil, soybean oil, highly-processed peanut butter, and shortening.

Similarly, toss the white flour; there are so many alternatives to it that offer so much more in the way of nutrition while achieving exactly the same purpose that there's just no point to keeping any white flour around. Get rid of the processed sugar as well, along with the processed syrups. And demote those multi-ingredient commercial crackers, packaged doughnuts, and similar snacks. These are precisely the foods you want to wean your kids away from if you're serious about giving them the benefits and joys of real food.

You'll open up passageways in your crowded refrigerator, too, if you eliminate a lot of dairy and discard any sort of fabricated lunch meats. If milk plays a crucial role in your diet, try plant-based and nut milks. If your family can't live without ice cream, check out fresh fruit gelato that is actually dairy-free. And if you eat cheese, buy organic or grass-fed and store only a small amount of it at a time. As to lunch meats—packaged baloney is "the classic"—try the real thing instead.

PANTRY MUST-HAVES

Your pantry holds the staples of cooking, the building blocks of a meal you can pull together under just about any circumstances. But because it is the essential go-to source, I find it helps if the pantry is (a) organized and (b) appealing enough that a peek inside gets your taste buds buzzing and stimulates your appetite.

I divide my kitchen's dry pantry into zones:

FLOURS & GRAINS

- **Gluten-free or whole-grain flours:** chickpea or coconut flour, and whole wheat or brown rice flours
- **Whole grains:** like rolled oats, farro, bulgur, and quinoa
- **Whole-grain rices:** basmati, wild, or black

CANNED ITEMS

- **Legumes:** including beans of various colors like black, red, white; as well as lentils like red, green, brown, Beluga black, French green
- **Canned fish:** tuna and salmon, obtained smartly and sustainably

OILS & VINEGARS

- **Healthier oils:** including olive oil, coconut oil, and nut oils
- **Vinegars:** black, rice, and chili vinegars. I keep chili vinegar on hand at all times to brighten a dish. (Get the recipe on page 235.)

HERBS & SPICES

- **Dried herbs and spices:** like turmeric and cumin
- **Teas:** organic, herbal, and green
- **Kosher salt and sea salts:** collected from various locations around the world

NUTS, SEEDS, & DRIED FRUIT

- **Nuts:** organic and dehydrated macadamias, pistachios, peanuts
- **Nut butters:** unsweetened natural almond butter, cashew butter, and more. (To make your own, see pages 232 and 234.)
- **Seeds:** flaxseeds, pumpkin, and sesame seeds
- **Dried fruit:** raisins, cherries, cranberries, apricots, peaches, and more. Take care to stick to organic or sulfite-free because some processors use sulfites as a preservative, which can cause allergic reactions.

SWEETENERS

- **Natural and minimally processed sweeteners:** raw honey, pure maple syrup, coconut sugar, and date sugar, which are better than the processed sugars

NECESSARY ACCESSORIES

- A zone devoted to those essentials you know you always need to have around. For me, that means aluminum-free baking powder, gluten-free baking soda, various organic extracts (vanilla, peppermint, more), canned coconut milk, pumpkin or squash puree, and organic tomatoes.

My pantry also has a special zone devoted to the healthy powerhouses (page 20) I rely on for both their nutritional value and because they add flavor and zest to so many dishes I make, as you'll see in the recipes in this book.

These days many of these basic ingredients are as available for purchase online or at your local supermarket as they are in health food stores or specialty markets.

HEALTHY POWERHOUSE INGREDIENTS

Spirulina

Chia Seeds

Goji Berries

Maca

SPIRULINA, the most commonly available and frequently used type of blue-green algae, is a super-rich nutrient that can boost immune function, increase your protein intake, and protect against liver problems. But before you introduce it into your diet, check with your doctor about how much you should consume. I buy it in powder form and sprinkle it in smoothies, vinaigrettes, and any dish that's green.

CHIA SEEDS are an import from the Andes. The seeds of this flowering plant from the mint family are great for lowering blood pressure and are very, very rich in omega-3s. Another plus as a cooking ingredient is that the seeds expand to hold 10 to 12 times their weight, so you don't need a lot of chia seeds to get bang for the buck.

GOJI BERRIES were originally cultivated in China where they are known as an antioxidant-packed, antiaging food and are routinely used in classic Chinese cuisine. The dried berries, which is what I keep in my pantry, are also said to have more beta-carotene than carrots and way more vitamin C than oranges, not to mention a bunch of compounds that boost the immune system. Their tart taste adds to their usefulness in a range of recipes, as you'll see in Quinoa-and-Vegetable Salad (page 66) and All the Way Up Energy Bars (page 120).

MACA is a root that grows high in the Andes, where, according to myth or tradition or both, Inca warriors used to consume large amounts of it before a battle. What's no myth is that maca has incredible nutritional value and is particularly rich in essential minerals. In powder form, it's another great smoothie ingredient as you'll see in Mango-and-Maca Smoothie (page 37), but anywhere you use it, it is bound to be a plus for your overall stamina and endurance.

THE 100% REAL-FOOD FRIDGE

Chances are you open your fridge way more times than you open your pantry, so it's even more important that it should offer a welcoming, even seductive scene to feast your eyes on. A fridge should not look drab. On the contrary, it should look as happy and healthy, as vibrant and interesting as you want your family to be from eating fresh, real food.

So where protein is concerned, you want to open the refrigerator door to a vista of organic and pasture-fed, grass-fed meat; fresh eggs; nitrate-free bacon; and fresh fish caught wild.

Got milk? Use organic whole milk if you truly love it, but try nut milks like cashew or almond milk—as well as hemp and coconut—and above all, make sure any milk you drink is unsweetened.

To add to the variety of local, organic fruits and vegetables and fresh herbs you bought this morning, keep on hand chilled bottles or jars of fermented pickles and sauerkrauts, salsa, and kombucha drinks. Not to mention, for taste, organic mustards and/or different Dijon mustards in a range of heat levels and tastes.

A low-sodium or organic chicken broth is a good bet to keep in the fridge, and the same goes for organic, gluten-free breads and pastries, and for gluten-free muffin or pancake batter.

Of course, every fridge has leftovers, but don't forget about "preludes"—for example, the basic grains you cook on Sunday that only need a few finishing touches to be a savory breakfast or a one-bowl meal throughout the week.

Fresh, organic, locally sourced, as close to nature as possible, free of junk and preservatives and synthetics—fill your fridge with these kinds of foods, and it will be an inviting place to visit and a reliable source of 100% real health and real taste for yourself and your family.

SAM'S GAME-CHANGING SUBSTITUTIONS

Here are some substitutions I use in place of the "traditional" choices for the staples of cooking and eating. Many of these subs are gluten-free, sugar-free, and dairy-free. You'll lose absolutely nothing in taste and will gain substantially in real-food goodness.

WHITE FLOUR	chickpea, coconut, and brown rice flours
SWEETENERS	coconut sugar, date sugar, maple syrup, and raw honey in place of processed sugars
CANOLA OIL	olive oil, coconut oil, grapeseed oil, and nut oils
CHEESE	butternut squash, avocado, and almond cheese
RED MEAT	mushrooms, chickpeas
DAIRY MILK	unsweetened almond, cashew, coconut, and hemp milks

EQUIPMENT ESSENTIALS

Everybody always wants to know about the special equipment we chefs rely on, as if the secret to gourmet cooking was in the tools we use. Well, maybe it is. So here is the Sam Talbot list of essential kitchen equipment. Ready?

YOU WILL NEED:
- an oven/stove
- a cutting board
- a blender and food processor (Vitamix or Cuisinart accepted)
- a (really good) knife
- a cast-iron skillet
- a four-quart saucepan
- a sauté pan (for searing, pan-roasting, braising, and all-around sauce-making as well)
- wooden skewers (six inches long)
- different-sized mixing bowls

It is not a big list, but trust me when I say that these items, plus friends and family, are all you need. With them, you're perfectly equipped to produce 100% real and 100% delicious meals for yourself and your family. You're welcome to stock up on any other equipment that catches your fancy, but honestly, these are all I ever need, and they're all you'll need for any of the recipes in this book.

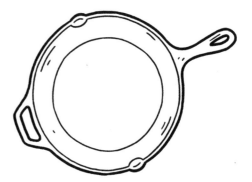

MORNING ESSENTIALS FOR THE GRIND

The morning meal really is the fuel for whatever the rest of the day brings, no matter your age or occupation. It is the way we humans boot up—how we initialize our physiological systems and processes, get our organs and nerves and muscles firing so we keep our edge all day. It is *the* crucial meal. We've seen what a difference it makes for school kids; start their day with the right balance of sufficient protein and sufficient grains, and their test scores go through the roof. And if you're the kind of workaholic who sometimes skips lunch, the right breakfast can keep your nose to the grindstone.

In the recipes that follow, for everything from smoothies that pack big-time energy and health into a single glass to beautifully plated sit-down breakfasts and brunches, I've aimed for both taste and the power to boot up your day.

These waffles can be made ahead and frozen. Just pop the frozen waffles into a toaster and you'll have breakfast all week.

WORLD'S FLUFFIEST WAFFLES

HANDS-ON: **15 MINUTES**   TOTAL: **15 MINUTES**   SERVES **6**   🟢 🟣

These waffles offer a pillow-soft texture that just doesn't happen with traditional white flour. Try it and you'll see what I mean.

1 cup (about 2 ounces) white rice flour

½ cup (about 1.62 ounces) chickpea flour

½ cup (about 2.13 ounces) tapioca flour

2 tablespoons coconut flour

½ cup chopped pecans

6 tablespoons coconut sugar

1 tablespoon ground cinnamon

1½ teaspoons baking powder

½ teaspoon sea salt

1 cup unsweetened hemp milk or almond milk

2 tablespoons applesauce

2 teaspoons orange zest

1 teaspoon pure vanilla extract

2 large eggs, separated

½ cup melted coconut oil, plus more for brushing waffle iron

Salted butter, softened

Pure maple syrup

1 Whisk together the flours, pecans, sugar, cinnamon, baking powder, and salt in a large bowl.

2 Whisk together the hemp milk, applesauce, orange zest, vanilla, egg yolks, and ½ cup of the melted coconut oil in a separate bowl.

3 Beat the egg whites with an electric mixer at high speed until soft peaks form, about 2 minutes.

4 Pour the milk mixture into the flour mixture, and gently stir until just incorporated. (It's okay if there are a few lumps.) Fold in the egg whites.

5 Pour about ½ cup of the batter for each waffle onto a preheated waffle iron brushed with melted coconut oil. Cook until the waffles are golden, about 2 ½ minutes. Transfer to a rimmed baking sheet, and keep warm in a 200°F oven. Top with softened butter and maple syrup.

RIPE BANANA-AND-DARK CHOCOLATE PANCAKES WITH MAPLE SYRUP AND COCONUT CREAM

HANDS-ON: **15 MINUTES**   TOTAL: **20 MINUTES**   SERVES **4**   GF V DF

These moist, flourless pancakes keep you feeling satisfied without the midmorning crash that refined carbs can cause. If you are sensitive to gluten, make sure to buy non-contaminated gluten-free oats.

1 (13.66-ounce) can coconut milk, chilled at least 4 hours

3 large eggs

Pinch of fine sea salt

3 ripe bananas, mashed

¾ cup uncooked quick-cooking oats

2 ounces bittersweet chocolate, grated, plus more for garnish

½ cup pure maple syrup, warmed

1 Without shaking or tilting the can, carefully open the coconut milk. Remove the solidified coconut cream from the top, and place in a chilled bowl. (Reserve the liquid for another use.) Beat the coconut cream with an electric mixer at high speed until stiff peaks form, about 4 minutes. Cover and chill until ready to serve.

2 Whisk together the eggs and salt in a medium bowl; whisk in the bananas, oats, and 2 ounces of the chocolate. Let the batter stand 5 minutes or until slightly thickened.

3 Pour about ¼ cup of the batter for each pancake onto a hot, lightly greased griddle or large nonstick skillet. Cook over medium-high until the edges appear dry and bubbles form on the surface, 2 to 3 minutes. Turn the pancakes over, and cook until firm and golden brown, about 2 more minutes. Serve the pancakes topped with the maple syrup and coconut cream. Garnish with the grated chocolate.

TIP

Want more coconut flavor? Sprinkle shredded coconut on the pancakes while cooking for extra texture.

SPICED FRENCH TOAST WITH ROASTED APRICOTS

HANDS-ON: **25 MINUTES**   TOTAL: **25 MINUTES**   SERVES **4**

French toast is a great, weekend brunch-worthy way to use day-old, leftover bread. No apricots? Sub in plums, nectarines, or cherries.

6 large eggs, beaten

2 cups unsweetened almond milk

2 teaspoons pure vanilla extract

1 teaspoon ground cinnamon

¼ teaspoon ground allspice

⅛ teaspoon freshly grated nutmeg

⅛ teaspoon ground cloves

¾ cup coconut sugar, plus more for serving

8 (1-inch-thick) whole-grain bread slices, preferably day-old

1 pound apricots, diced

⅛ teaspoon fine sea salt

½ cup plain Greek yogurt

2 tablespoons coconut oil, at room temperature (solid)

4 teaspoons puffed quinoa

1 Whisk together the eggs, almond milk, vanilla, cinnamon, allspice, nutmeg, cloves, and ½ cup of the coconut sugar. Place the bread in a 13- x 9-inch baking dish, and pour the egg mixture over the bread. Let stand, flipping the bread once or twice, until the bread is fully saturated, about 10 minutes.

2 Cook the apricots, salt, and the remaining ¼ cup of the coconut sugar in a medium saucepan over medium until the apricots are soft and sweet, and the juices have released, about 10 minutes. Pour the mixture through a fine wire-mesh strainer; return the cooking liquid to the saucepan, and reserve the apricots. Bring the cooking liquid to a boil over medium-high; boil until the mixture is syrupy and reduced to about 3 tablespoons, 5 to 7 minutes. Stir 1 tablespoon of the syrup into the yogurt; reserve the remaining syrup.

3 Melt 1 tablespoon of the coconut oil in a large nonstick skillet over medium-high. Add 4 of the bread slices, and cook until browned on each side, about 2 to 3 minutes per side. Repeat with the remaining 1 tablespoon coconut oil and remaining 4 bread slices.

4 Place 2 slices of the French toast on each of 4 plates; top with the reserved apricots. Dollop each serving with 2 tablespoons of the yogurt mixture, and top with 1 teaspoon of the puffed quinoa. Drizzle with the reserved syrup, and sprinkle with coconut sugar.

AVOCADO-AND-MELON MORNING LASSI

HANDS-ON: **10 MINUTES**   TOTAL: **10 MINUTES**   SERVES **4**   GF V

If you think of lassi as dessert or some cloyingly sweet version of a sugary yogurt drink, think again. This lassi starts with the superfruit avocado, filled with essential fats and vitamins, then adds the naturally sweet melon to cut the fat and quench your thirst—without a hint of fat or cholesterol. Try goat's-milk yogurt or add 1 teaspoon spirulina for a healthier twist.

1 ripe avocado

1 cup chopped seasonal melon, preferably honeydew

1 cup ice cubes

1 cup unsweetened almond milk or hemp milk

½ cup plain yogurt (not Greek-style)

¼ cup pure maple syrup

2 tablespoons fresh lemon or lime juice

1 tablespoon chopped fresh ginger

⅛ teaspoon fine sea salt, optional

Process the avocado, melon, ice, milk, yogurt, maple syrup, lemon or lime juice, and ginger in a blender until smooth and creamy. Taste the lassi, and add the sea salt, if desired.

TIP

You can make this lassi the night before; just keep it refrigerated, and serve it chilled.

MANGO-AND-MACA SMOOTHIE

HANDS-ON: **15 MINUTES**   TOTAL: **15 MINUTES**   SERVES **4**   (GF) (DF) (VG)

Does it get any better than mango and maca in the morning? The combined fragrance of these two superfoods, both intoxicating and enticing, really gets you going first thing, setting just the right tone for the rest of the day. But we're also talking about a major-league, all-natural, total stamina-and-endurance builder. Maca, after all, is grown and ground at the summit of the highest mountains in the Peruvian Andes, so this smoothie has major swag. This smoothie is best consumed really cold and as soon as it's made, but if you have any leftover, let it sit in the fridge for a bit so the maca flavor intensifies even further.

3 cups unsweetened hemp milk

½ cup ice cubes

⅓ cup fresh lemon juice (about 2 lemons)

3 ripe fresh mangoes, peeled and coarsely chopped

2 ounces dried mango

1 tablespoon almond butter

1 tablespoon flaxseeds

1 teaspoon maca powder

1 teaspoon pure vanilla extract

2 pitted dates

Pinch of Himalayan salt

Process all ingredients in a blender until smooth and creamy.

BLUEBERRY-POMEGRANATE SMOOTHIE

HANDS-ON: **10 MINUTES**   TOTAL: **10 MINUTES**   SERVES **4**   GF   V

Both blueberries and pomegranates are packed with antioxidants.

2 cups frozen blueberries

1 cup 100% pomegranate juice, chilled

1 tablespoon raw honey

1 (6-ounce) carton vanilla or plain yogurt (not Greek-style)

Process the blueberries, pomegranate juice, honey, and yogurt in a blender until smooth. Serve immediately.

TIP

Sprinkle in maca powder or chia seeds for an extra boost of nutrients.

JUICING 101:
QUICK "-ADE" FOR HEALTH AND FLAVOR, ANY TIME OF DAY

THESE DAYS it almost seems like there is a juice bar on every corner. Fresh juice helps you get more fruits and vegetables into your daily routine, gives you an antioxidant boost, and keeps you hydrated. Make your own juice and experiment with different combos to find a few favorites. All it takes is a blender and your creativity.

You know all about lemonade, don't you? It's made of real lemon juice, maybe some water or club soda, and—unless you intend to walk around all day with puckered lips—some form of sweetener. Expand on that formula with just about any fruit or vegetable with high water content, and you've got yourself a health "ade" you can put together quickly and easily. No, it is not the traditional "glass of juice," but it is an instant jolt of health, and it's delicious.

Multiply the number of fruits or vegetables, or mix them together: watermelon + cucumber + apple + orange, for example. Add a squeeze of lime juice to the mix, spritz in some club soda or seltzer, and now you're ready for a bit of sweetener—namely, any of the many natural alternatives to processed sugar I use in the recipes in this book. But pureed apple also fits the sweetening bill, as does pureed pineapple. And I recommend hibiscus. Simultaneously sweet and tart, it also adds a reddish hue to your whatever-ade. Hibiscus-apple-and-celery-ade, anyone?

ORANGE-HONEY-ADE

SERVES **4**

Try this when your immune system needs a vitaman C boost.

1 cup fresh orange juice (about 3 oranges)
⅓ cup fresh lime juice (about 3 limes)
⅓ cup blossom honey
Zest of 1 orange
2 to 3 sprigs of fresh mint
3 cups soda water or water
Lime wedges, for serving

Combine the citrus juices and honey with a whisk or in a blender. Add the zest, mint, and soda water. Let chill 1 to 2 hours. Serve over ice with a wedge of lime.

WATERMELON-ADE

SERVES **5**

Hydration made better.

4 cups chopped seedless watermelon
1 cup pineapple
¼ cup fresh lemon juice (from 2 lemons)
¼ cup raw honey
2 cups soda water or water
Lime slices, for serving

Process all the ingredients in a blender until smooth. Let chill for 1 to 2 hours. Serve over ice with a slice of lime.

AVOCADO TOAD-in-a-HOLE with BAKED HAM and SALSA VERDE

HANDS-ON: **25 MINUTES** TOTAL: **45 MINUTES** SERVES **4** 🄶🄵 🄳🄵

I love taking a whole avocado and cracking an egg in it. It is a fun, healthy take on the classic toast-and-egg recipe.

8 ounces tomatillos, husked, rinsed, and quartered

1 small yellow or white onion, quartered

2 garlic cloves, smashed

1 medium jalapeño chile, halved, seeds removed

3 tablespoons fresh lime juice (about 2 limes)

⅓ cup chopped fresh cilantro

1 teaspoon fine sea salt

2 ripe avocados

¼ teaspoon black pepper

4 medium eggs

1 teaspoon olive oil

8 ounces diced baked ham

1 Preheat the broiler with the oven rack 6 inches from the heat. Line 2 rimmed baking sheets with aluminum foil. Spread the tomatillos, onion, garlic, and jalapeño on 1 prepared baking sheet. Broil until blistered and lightly charred, 4 to 5 minutes on each side. Remove from the oven, and cool 20 minutes. Reduce the heat to 425°F.

2 Process the charred vegetables, lime juice, and ¼ cup of the cilantro in a food processor until smooth. Transfer to a bowl, and stir in ¾ teaspoon of the salt. Chill until ready to use.

3 Cut each avocado in half; remove and discard the pits. (To keep the avocados level, slice about ¼ inch from the back of the avocado halves so they will sit flat.) Enlarge the hole by scooping ⅛ to ¼ inch of flesh from around the hole. (Save the scooped avocado for another use.) Sprinkle the avocados with the black pepper and remaining ¼ teaspoon salt; place on a second foil-lined, rimmed baking sheet.

4 Bake at 425°F until no residual moisture remains in the hole, about 8 minutes. Remove from oven. Working with 1 egg at a time, break the eggs into a bowl, and, using the eggshell, scoop 1 yolk into each hot avocado. Add enough egg white to fill the hole completely. (Discard the remaining egg whites.) Cover the avocados with foil, and return to the oven. Bake until the whites are set and the yolks are runny, about 5 minutes.

5 Meanwhile, heat a medium skillet over medium-high, and add the olive oil and diced ham; cook until browned and the edges are crispy, about 4 minutes. Sprinkle the avocado halves with the crispy ham and remaining chopped cilantro. Serve with the salsa verde.

You can double up on the salsa verde and keep it in the fridge for up to 1 week.

SOUFFLÉ OMELET with SWISS CHARD and MIXED HERBS

HANDS-ON: **20 MINUTES**   TOTAL: **30 MINUTES**   SERVES **4**   GF V

This good-looking spin on a frittata makes for a quick company-worthy brunch dish or a super simple dinner. Substitute kale or spinach for the chard.

8 ounces Swiss chard

2 tablespoons extra-virgin olive oil

2 tablespoons finely chopped shallots

1 cup sliced cremini mushrooms

¾ teaspoon sea salt

½ teaspoon black pepper

5 large eggs, separated

¼ ounce Parmigiano-Reggiano cheese, finely grated with a Microplane grater (about ¼ cup)

2 tablespoons torn fresh basil

2 tablespoons torn fresh flat-leaf parsley

2 tablespoons torn fresh chives

1 Preheat the oven to 425°F. Remove the stems from the Swiss chard, and reserve for another use. Chop the Swiss chard leaves, and set aside.

2 Heat 1 tablespoon of the olive oil in a large ovenproof nonstick skillet over medium. Add the shallots, and cook, stirring often, until translucent, about 3 minutes. Add the mushrooms, and increase the heat to medium-high. Cook the mushrooms until they release their liquid and brown lightly, about 7 minutes. Add the Swiss chard leaves, ½ teaspoon of the salt, and ¼ teaspoon of the pepper; cook until the leaves are wilted, about 1 minute. Remove from the heat; transfer the mixture to a bowl, and wipe the skillet clean with paper towels.

3 Beat the egg whites with an electric mixer at high speed until stiff peaks form, 3 to 4 minutes. Whisk together the egg yolks and remaining ¼ teaspoon each salt and pepper in a separate bowl. Using a spatula, carefully fold the egg whites into the yolks just until combined.

4 Heat the remaining 1 tablespoon oil in the skillet over medium. Spread the egg mixture evenly in the skillet. Cook until a crust begins to form, about 30 seconds. Sprinkle with the vegetable mixture and cheese.

5 Bake at 425°F until the omelet has risen and looks puffy, about 3 minutes. Using a spatula, carefully transfer the omelet to a cutting board. Sprinkle with the basil, parsley, and chives, and cut into 8 wedges. Serve immediately.

BLACK BEAN, POBLANO, AND FRIED EGG TOSTADAS

HANDS-ON: **30 MINUTES**   TOTAL: **30 MINUTES**   SERVES **4**   GF V

A delicious and savory take on huevos rancheros that works just about anytime of day. You can use store-bought tostada shells instead of frying your own.

1 (15-ounce) can black beans, undrained

2 teaspoons fresh lime juice (from 1 lime)

½ teaspoon fine sea salt

3 ½ tablespoons coconut oil, at room temperature (solid)

1 poblano chile, stems and seeds removed, thinly sliced

1 cup thinly sliced red onion

1 tablespoon ground cumin

8 (6-inch) yellow corn tortillas

8 large eggs

½ cup pico de gallo

¼ cup loosely packed cilantro leaves

1 ounce queso fresco (fresh Mexican cheese), crumbled (about ¼ cup)

1 ripe avocado, thinly sliced

Lime wedges, for serving

1 Drain the black beans, reserving ¼ cup of the liquid from the can. Combine the beans and reserved liquid in a small saucepan; bring to a boil over medium-high. Cook, stirring often, until the beans are heated through, about 2 minutes. Mash the beans coarsely with a potato masher. Stir in the lime juice and ¼ teaspoon of the salt. Remove from the heat, and cover to keep warm.

2 Melt 1 tablespoon of the coconut oil in a large nonstick skillet over medium-high. Add the poblano and red onion; cook until tender and lightly browned, 7 to 8 minutes. Sprinkle with the cumin and remaining ¼ teaspoon salt; cook, stirring often, until fragrant, about 1 minute. Wipe the skillet clean.

3 Melt 1 tablespoon of the coconut oil in the skillet over medium-high. Fry the tortillas, 2 at a time, until crisp and golden brown, about 2 minutes per side, and add 1 tablespoon of the coconut oil after the second batch. Transfer the crisp tortillas to a wire rack.

4 Reduce the heat to medium-low, and melt the remaining ½ tablespoon coconut oil in the skillet; break the eggs into the skillet, and cook until the eggs detach from the bottom of the skillet, 2 to 3 minutes. Remove from the heat; cover and let stand until the whites are set and the yolks are still runny, about 2 minutes. Carefully transfer the eggs to a cutting board, and separate them gently with a knife.

5 Spread 2 tablespoons of the bean mixture on each tostada. Top with 1 tablespoon of the poblano mixture and 1 egg. Serve with the pico de gallo, cilantro, queso fresco, avocado slices, and lime wedges.

SMOKY HARISSA-AND-ROASTED RED PEPPER SHAKSHUKA

HANDS-ON: **35 MINUTES**   TOTAL: **40 MINUTES**   SERVES **6**   GF V

Poaching eggs in sauce might sound tricky, but this flavor-packed recipe is crazy easy to make. Spicy, smoky, and oh-so-satisfying, shakshuka should be on your must-try list.

2 red bell peppers

2 tablespoons olive oil

1 large yellow onion, thinly sliced

3 garlic cloves, minced

1 tablespoon smoked paprika

1 teaspoon cumin seeds

1 (28-ounce) can tomato puree

2 tablespoons harissa

¾ teaspoon sea salt

¼ teaspoon black pepper

6 large eggs

1 ½ ounces crumbled feta cheese (about ⅓ cup)

2 tablespoons torn fresh flat-leaf parsley

Toasted flatbread or pita rounds

1 Preheat the broiler with the oven rack 6 inches from the heat. Broil the peppers in an aluminum foil-lined rimmed baking sheet, turning occasionally, until charred allover, 13 to 15 minutes. Transfer the peppers to a bowl, and cover with plastic wrap; let stand until the skins are loosened, about 15 minutes. Peel the peppers; remove and discard the stems and seeds. Cut the peppers into strips.

2 Heat the olive oil in a large deep skillet over medium. Add the onion, and cook, stirring occasionally, until the onions begin to caramelize, about 15 minutes. Add the garlic, smoked paprika, and cumin seeds; cook, stirring constantly, until fragrant, about 1 minute. Stir in the sliced peppers, tomato puree, harissa, salt, and pepper. Increase the heat to medium-high, and bring to a boil; reduce the heat to medium-low.

3 Carefully crack the eggs, and slip them into the sauce, making sure the yolks do not break. Return the mixture to a simmer. Cover and cook until the egg whites are just cooked but the yolks are slightly runny, 4 to 5 minutes. Sprinkle with the feta and parsley. Serve with the toasted flatbread or pita rounds.

TIP

Roasted peppers can be made ahead and stored in the fridge for up to 1 week.

SAVORY PORRIDGE WITH BABY KALE, WILD MUSHROOMS, AND HAZELNUTS

HANDS-ON: **35 MINUTES**   TOTAL: **45 MINUTES**   SERVES **2**   (GF) (DF) (VG)

Think of this as a breakfast risotto. You can make a large batch and keep it stored in the refrigerator for up to a week. Simply add a little more almond milk or stock when reheating.

2 ¾ cups vegetable stock

1 cup unsweetened almond milk

¾ cup uncooked steel-cut oats

¾ teaspoon kosher salt

2 tablespoons extra-virgin olive oil

½ cup sliced shallots

1 teaspoon chopped fresh thyme

1 teaspoon pure maple syrup

4 ounces sliced mixed wild mushrooms (such as cremini, oyster, and shiitake)

2 cups firmly packed baby kale

½ cup blanched hazelnuts, toasted and coarsely chopped

Fresh thyme leaves

1 Combine the vegetable stock and almond milk in a medium saucepan, and bring to a boil over medium-high. Stir in the oats and ½ teaspoon of the salt, and return to a boil. Reduce the heat to medium-low to maintain a gentle simmer, and cook until tender and creamy, about 30 to 40 minutes, adding more vegetable stock or almond milk, if desired.

2 Meanwhile, heat 1 tablespoon of the extra-virgin olive oil in a medium nonstick skillet over medium. Add the shallots, chopped thyme, and remaining ¼ teaspoon salt; cook until sizzling, about 2 minutes. Reduce the heat to medium-low, and cook, stirring occasionally, until the shallots are deep golden brown and very soft, about 30 minutes. Stir in the maple syrup, and cook 2 more minutes. Remove the shallot mixture, and coarsely chop.

3 Add the mushrooms and remaining 1 tablespoon oil to the skillet; increase the heat to medium-high, and cook, stirring occasionally, until browned and tender, 6 to 8 minutes. Add the baby kale, and cook until wilted, about 1 minute.

4 Stir the mushroom mixture, shallot mixture, and ¼ cup of the hazelnuts into the oatmeal mixture. Divide among 2 bowls, and top with the remaining ¼ cup hazelnuts. Garnish with the fresh thyme leaves.

HONEY CRUNCH GRANOLA WITH BLUEBERRY, COCONUT, AND LIME

HANDS-ON: **10 MINUTES**   TOTAL: **1 HOUR, 30 MINUTES**   SERVES **10**   GF DF V

Granola has to be one of the most popular breakfast and snack foods of all time. But exercise caution when you buy your supply. Store shelves often feature some really sad excuses for granola, much of it riddled with tons of sugar or corn syrup. With this recipe, we keep it real. Mad coconut. Mad blueberries. Mad love.

- 3 cups uncooked regular rolled oats
- ⅔ cup hulled pumpkin seeds (pepitas)
- ⅔ cup dried unsweetened blueberries
- ½ cup unsweetened dried coconut
- ½ cup (about 2 ounces) coconut flour
- ⅓ cup white sesame seeds
- 1 ½ teaspoons sea salt
- ½ cup coconut oil, at room temperature (solid)
- ½ cup raw honey
- 1 ½ tablespoons lime zest, plus ¼ cup fresh juice (from about 2 limes)

1 Preheat the oven to 325°F. Stir together the oats, pumpkin seeds, blueberries, dried coconut, coconut flour, sesame seeds, and salt in a large bowl.

2 Melt the oil with the honey and lime juice in a small saucepan over medium-low, stirring often; bring to a simmer. Pour over the oat mixture, and stir until well combined and the oat mixture is fully coated.

3 Spread the granola in 2 large rimmed baking sheets, and bake at 325°F on the upper third and lower third racks until golden brown, about 20 minutes, stirring once halfway through. Cool completely in the pans on wire racks, about 1 hour. Stir the lime zest into the cooled granola.

TIP

This granola will last for 2 weeks in an airtight container and at cool room temperature. Serve it with your favorite milk or yogurt, or atop a fruit crumble.

2

SANDWICHES, SALADS, AND SPREADS: ARTISANAL AND ACCESSIBLE

Today, even a so-called "casual" lifestyle is on the go, but between the thousand things to do and the hundred places to get to in order to do them, it's nice to find some stability. These sandwiches, salads, and spreads answer the demands for good health and great taste as well as for being at-the-ready when you need them. Any and all can serve as the foundation for brown-bagging your lunch, for a day trip with no particular destination in mind, for a weeklong camping trip in the wild, or to store in the fridge for the guest who shows up unexpectedly. Indulge the artisan in you, and easily access the results.

SPRING PEA-AND-MINT SPREAD

HANDS-ON: **10 MINUTES**   TOTAL: **10 MINUTES**   MAKES **1 ¾ CUPS**   GF DF VG

This is a quick and easy spread that is fresh and colorful to enjoy with crudités or gluten-free crackers. Try it as a condiment for vegetarian wrap sandwiches as well.

2 cups blanched fresh or thawed frozen English peas

2 to 3 tablespoons olive oil

1 teaspoon kosher salt

½ teaspoon ground white pepper

¼ cup chopped fresh mint

1 tablespoon lemon zest, plus 2 tablespoons fresh juice (from 1 lemon)

Process all ingredients in a food processor until smooth, about 1 minute. Add additional salt and pepper, if desired.

TIP
Try making this spread using edamame or butter beans.

BUY SEASONAL, BUY LOCAL

IT'S A TWO-PART mantra that can't be repeated too often: buy fresh foods in season, and buy them from local sources. Make these foods the centerpiece of your eating, and you can't go wrong in terms of either health or taste.

On the health side of the equation, the reason is as simple as it is obvious: the closer a food is to having been harvested—in terms of both time and geography—the more powerful its content of textures and nutrients and the more effectively it can combat disease and improve your health. The taste side of the equation is equally obvious: comparing the taste of a just-picked peach or winter squash or asparagus stalk to its canned, jarred, or packaged equivalent, typically "preserved" by added and often synthetic ingredients, is a little like comparing Lil Kickers soccer to the World Cup final. They're not only not in the same league; it's like they're not really playing the same game.

Mostly, to be sure, buying fresh and buying local means shopping for your food in farmers' markets whenever you can. There was a time when the only people who frequented farmers' markets were chefs like me, but that's no longer the case. These days, such markets are so popular they've become tourist destinations! What's more, they're everywhere, and they're open all year round. If you're not aware of one near you, check out the U.S. Department of Agriculture's list at www.ams.usda.gov/local-food-directories/farmersmarkets. Chances are good there's at least one you can get to as easily as to a supermarket.

Of course, what's available at the farmers' market will change with the season and depends on the climate and soil conditions of your region of the country. And that's precisely the point: seasonal and regional variety is your assurance that you're getting only what's locally grown and as fresh as it can be. Besides, such variety helps provide an adventure and ignite creativity, and great eating should do both. For me personally, I love the progression from summer's bounty of fresh berries and melons and corn and lots of choice, through autumn's root vegetables and gourds and Brussels sprouts and kale, into potatoes and carrots and cabbage and squashes through the winter as I begin to rev up my appetite for the first fruits of spring's gardens.

In some places—mostly big cities—the local farmers' market is open every day. Elsewhere, the market may be open only one or two days a week. My advice, whenever you go, is to enter the market without preconceived menus, then just start off with a "window-shopping" lap to see what's available, compare prices, check out the variety, and get some ideas. Bring this book along with you so you can match what's on offer at the market with some recipes.

One important note: the produce in these farmers' markets can be so alluring that I invariably see people stocking up like crazy. There's a danger in that; if you buy too much, you may end up throwing some of it away, which would be a shame. So buy only what you need for the few days or week until the market is open again.

If there really is no farmers' market near you, try for produce that's as seasonal and local as possible in your local supermarket. Yes,

we all know that, traditionally, supermarkets are expressly designed to keep the fresh food peripheral and push us toward items with a higher profit margin. The path to the back of the store or the sidelines, where produce tends to reside, is booby-trapped with seductive displays and discount pricing to get us to buy stuff we don't need and probably don't even want. This seems to be changing in many places where a number of savvy supermarkets are coming around to the view that fresh produce, beautifully displayed, is increasingly a draw. In fact, more and more supermarkets are making a point of getting their supplies from local farmers, and many establishments today block out an area of the produce section for local foods.

But if you're still stuck with the traditional supermarket that forces you to trudge down aisle after aisle before you get to the produce, keep a few truths in mind. First of all, produce deliveries tend to arrive during the week, Monday through Friday, so that's when you want to shop. Also, it's customary to place the newer produce arrivals in the back of the display so that the older merchandise will sell first. It means you'll need to reach back or dig deep to find the freshest. Also, don't forget that you can—and should—talk to the produce manager and find out what is freshest and where the produce is sourced from. If they don't already source locally, suggest it. (And by the way, local, regional, or smaller-brand "gourmet" packaged foods, often in the real-food category, tend to be on the very top shelves of the supermarket, so heads up!)

In the farmers' market or a supermarket, of course, touch and smell any produce you're interested in buying. Fresh food is firm, heavier than food that's been sitting around losing water, preferably unbruised, and smells of the flavor within.

It's hard to go wrong with fresh ingredients prepared simply.

STRAWBERRY-AND-PEA SHOOT SALAD WITH ROASTED GINGER AND CHILI VINEGAR

HANDS-ON: **20 MINUTES**   TOTAL: **20 MINUTES**   SERVES **4**   (GF) (DF) (VG)

This salad is composed like a delicate serenade, but then the mixture of toasted seeds, roasted ginger, and a ton of fresh herbs gives it the needed crescendo to sustain the hungriest salad eaters. The strawberries must be in season and überfresh. Fun to make, with big flavor and big color, this recipe defines seasonal perfection.

2 tablespoons sesame oil

1 tablespoon grated fresh ginger

2 teaspoons finely chopped fresh lemongrass

3 tablespoons roasted garlic olive oil

½ teaspoon lime zest, plus 2 tablespoons fresh juice (from 2 limes)

½ teaspoon fine sea salt

¼ teaspoon black pepper

¼ teaspoon chili vinegar (or make your own, page 235)

1 cup chopped fresh strawberries

4 tablespoons hulled pumpkin seeds (pepitas)

2 tablespoons black sesame seeds

1 tablespoon coconut sugar

4 ounces (about 2 cups) pea tendrils or shoots

½ cup torn fresh basil or Thai basil

½ cup torn fresh cilantro

1 Heat the sesame oil in a large skillet over medium-high. Add the ginger and lemongrass; cook, stirring often, until fragrant, about 3 minutes. Remove from the heat.

2 Whisk together the roasted garlic olive oil, zest, juice, salt, pepper, and vinegar in a bowl. Add the strawberries and sesame oil mixture; stir gently to combine.

3 Combine the pumpkin seeds, sesame seeds, and coconut sugar in a cast-iron skillet over medium-high. Cook until fragrant and the seeds are toasted, 4 to 5 minutes.

4 Gently toss together the pea tendrils, basil, and cilantro in a bowl. Add 1 tablespoon of the roasted garlic oil vinaigrette from the strawberry mixture to the pea tendril mixture; gently toss to coat.

5 Divide the pea tendril mixture among 4 plates. Top with the strawberry mixture. Sprinkle with the pumpkin seed mixture.

SPICY END-of-SUMMER MELON SALAD

HANDS-ON: **15 MINUTES**   TOTAL: **15 MINUTES**   SERVES **4**   (GF) (V) (DF)

In the Northeast, as my summers on Long Island and in Maine have taught me, melons keep ripening late into the season. One fall day in a coastal farmers' market, I bought up the last six melons available and turned them into this salad— simultaneously sweet and sharp, blending summer right into fall. A delicious and exciting way to end the season.

1 to 2 small melons, scooped into balls to equal 3 cups

1 cup firmly packed mixed baby greens

¼ cup fresh pineapple juice

1 to 1 ½ tablespoons chili vinegar (or make your own, page 235)

1 tablespoon olive oil

1 tablespoon raw honey

1 teaspoon lemon zest

¼ teaspoon ground cumin

¼ teaspoon red chile flakes

¼ teaspoon ground cinnamon

12 to 15 small fresh mint leaves, torn

¼ teaspoon fine sea salt

Gently toss together all ingredients in a large bowl.

SNAP SALAD WITH STRAWBERRIES, SPEARMINT, AND LEMONGRASS

HANDS-ON: **19 MINUTES**   TOTAL: **19 MINUTES**   SERVES **4**   GF V DF

Lemongrass is one of my favorite ingredients. It has a bright citrusy flavor and is packed with health benefits. Store it in the fridge, loosely wrapped in plastic, and remove the tough outer leaves before slicing.

1 stalk fresh lemongrass

1 tablespoon finely chopped shallot

1 tablespoon seeds removed and finely chopped serrano chile

1 tablespoon white wine vinegar

2 teaspoons raw honey

½ teaspoon fine sea salt

¼ teaspoon black pepper

3 tablespoons extra-virgin olive oil

1 pound snap peas, trimmed

1 cup halved small strawberries

1 cup pea shoots or watercress

3 tablespoons fresh spearmint leaves

1 Cut the top off the lemongrass, leaving the bottom 4 inches of stalk. Discard the top. Peel the lemongrass, and finely chop. Combine the chopped lemongrass, shallot, chile, vinegar, honey, salt, and black pepper in a small bowl. Slowly whisk in the oil. Set aside.

2 Fill a large Dutch oven with water, and bring to a boil over high. Add the snap peas; cook until tender-crisp, 45 seconds to 1 minute. Remove the peas, and plunge them into ice water to stop the cooking process; drain well.

3 Combine the peas, strawberries, pea shoots, and spearmint in a bowl. Add the vinaigrette; toss well to combine.

Try creamy sheep's milk ricotta for a hint of sweetness.

MARINATED MELON WITH SQUASH, RICOTTA, AND ARUGULA

HANDS-ON: **20 MINUTES**   TOTAL: **1 HOUR**   SERVES **4**   **GF**   **V**

One day in late fall, I went to a farmers' market on the Maine coast and picked up a ripe canary melon, a wonderful early winter squash, fresh arugula, and a beautiful ricotta from local cheesemonger Lakin's Gorges. Got it all home and was inspired to create this dish in which every ingredient can be heard and where each complements the others.

5 tablespoons olive oil

1 cup thinly sliced delicata squash or thinly sliced peeled butternut squash

⅓ cup diced red onion

⅓ cup diced shallot

3 garlic cloves, minced

1 teaspoon fennel seeds, toasted and ground

2 cups cubed melon

¼ cup red wine vinegar

¼ cup thinly sliced fresh basil

2 tablespoons thinly sliced fresh oregano

3 cups loosely packed arugula

2 teaspoons lemon zest, plus 2 tablespoons fresh juice (from 1 lemon)

⅛ teaspoon black pepper

¼ teaspoon fine sea salt

4 ounces ricotta cheese (about ½ cup)

1 Heat 2 tablespoons of the oil in a large skillet over medium-high. Add the squash, onion, shallot, garlic, and fennel seeds. Cook 3 minutes. Reduce the heat to medium, and cook until the vegetables are tender-crisp, about 5 minutes.

2 Combine the melon, vinegar, and remaining 3 tablespoons oil in a large mixing bowl. Chill 30 minutes. Remove from refrigerator, and let the mixture return to room temperature, about 30 minutes. Toss with the basil and oregano.

3 Toss the arugula with the lemon juice. Sprinkle with the pepper and ⅛ teaspoon of the salt.

4 Arrange the squash mixture, melon mixture, arugula, and ricotta on a large serving platter. Sprinkle with the zest and remaining ⅛ teaspoon salt.

QUINOA-AND-VEGETABLE SALAD WITH SHERRY VINAIGRETTE

HANDS-ON: **25 MINUTES**   TOTAL: **30 MINUTES**   SERVES **4**   Ⓥ ⒹⒻ

Fresh, crunchy, and earthy—this is a colorful salad that can be served on its own or with grilled shrimp or chicken. The red quinoa lends pretty color, but regular quinoa also works here.

1 ½ cups water

½ teaspoon kosher salt

1 cup uncooked red quinoa

1 tablespoon lemon zest, plus 2 tablespoons fresh juice (from 1 lemon)

¼ cup plus 1 teaspoon olive oil

4 cups firmly packed baby arugula

1 cup grated peeled carrots

1 cup grated peeled parsnips

½ cup thinly sliced celery

½ cup thinly sliced English cucumber

¼ cup dried goji berries

¼ cup golden raisins

2 tablespoons sherry vinegar

1 tablespoon Dijon mustard

1 teaspoon raw honey

½ teaspoon black pepper

½ cup toasted slivered almonds

1 Bring 1½ cups water and ¼ teaspoon of the salt to a boil in a medium saucepan over high. Stir in the quinoa, and reduce the heat to medium-low. Cover and simmer until done, about 15 minutes. Remove from the heat, and let stand 5 minutes. Fluff with a fork, and stir in the zest, juice, and 1 teaspoon of the oil. Set aside.

2 Toss together the arugula, carrots, parsnips, celery, cucumber, goji berries, and raisins in a large bowl. Whisk together the vinegar, mustard, honey, pepper, remaining ¼ cup oil, and remaining ¼ teaspoon salt in a small bowl. Drizzle the vinegar mixture over the arugula mixture in the large bowl; toss to coat.

3 Place about 2 ½ cups of the salad into each of 4 bowls; top with about ⅔ cup of the quinoa mixture. Sprinkle each with 2 tablespoons almonds.

RAW MUSHROOM SALAD WITH SESAME-GINGER BROWN BUTTER

HANDS-ON: **15 MINUTES**   TOTAL: **15 MINUTES**   SERVES **4**   Ⓥ

A friend asked me to invent something new for his restaurant, and sitting right there on the table in his kitchen was an assortment of different mushrooms. They inspired this dish, and when it was served to customers that night, it was such a hit my buddy put it on the permanent menu. The brown, salty butter brings all the tastes together and puts this salad over the top.

1 ½ pounds fresh mushrooms of various types (such as king, cremini, shiitake, and baby portobellos), stems removed and reserved for another use, quartered

2 tablespoons olive oil

2 tablespoons chili vinegar (or make your own, page 235)

2 tablespoons bottled yuzu juice

1 small jalapeño chile, shaved paper-thin on a mandoline

1 teaspoon fine sea salt

½ teaspoon black pepper

3 tablespoons unsalted butter, softened

2 tablespoons thinly sliced pickled ginger

1 tablespoon black sesame seeds

1 garlic clove, grated using a Microplane grater

2 tablespoons chopped fresh chives

1 Combine the mushrooms, oil, vinegar, yuzu juice, jalapeño slices, salt, and pepper in a large bowl.

2 Heat the butter in a cast-iron skillet over medium-high until foamy, 4 to 5 minutes. Add the ginger, sesame seeds, and garlic; cook until fragrant and slightly browned, 2 to 3 minutes.

3 Spoon the hot butter mixture over the mushrooms, and toss once. Sprinkle with the chives, and serve immediately.

WHITE BEAN-AND-CILANTRO HUMMUS

HANDS-ON: **10 MINUTES**   TOTAL: **10 MINUTES, PLUS CHILLING**   MAKES **3 CUPS**

This smooth and flavorful no-cook hummus can do double duty as a spread or the filling for a quick vegetarian sandwich. Add it to a pita or wrap with chopped tomatoes, cucumbers, carrots, and feta.

2 (14.5-ounce) cans no-salt-added cannellini beans, drained and rinsed

¼ cup tahini (sesame paste)

¼ cup vegetable broth or water

3 tablespoons fresh cilantro leaves

1 tablespoon white balsamic vinegar

1 tablespoon fresh lemon juice (from 1 lemon)

2 garlic cloves, minced

¼ teaspoon ground cumin

1 teaspoon fine sea salt

Process all ingredients in a food processor until smooth, about 1 minute. Cover and chill at least 30 minutes before serving.

ROASTED TOMATO-and-RED PEPPER ROMESCO

HANDS-ON: **10 MINUTES**   TOTAL: **30 MINUTES**   MAKES **1 ¾ CUPS**   (GF) (DF) (VG)

This riff on classic romesco has multiple culinary possibilities. Serve with crudités or gluten-free crackers, use as a sauce for pizzas, as a sandwich condiment, or even whisk into a quick vinaigrette for a salad.

2 cups grape tomatoes

1 medium-size red bell pepper, seeds removed, cut into 2-inch pieces

1 small red onion, quartered

2 garlic cloves, smashed

1 teaspoon kosher salt

1 teaspoon black pepper

2 tablespoons extra-virgin olive oil

1 cup toasted walnut halves

¼ cup roughly chopped fresh chives

1 tablespoon fresh lemon juice (from 1 lemon)

2 teaspoons sherry vinegar

1 teaspoon sweet Hungarian paprika

1 Preheat the oven to 450°F. Toss together the tomatoes, bell pepper, onion, garlic, salt, black pepper, and 1 tablespoon of the oil in a bowl. Arrange in a single layer on an aluminum foil-lined rimmed baking sheet. Bake in the preheated oven until the tomatoes are lightly charred and the juices have thickened on the baking sheet, 20 to 30 minutes.

2 Combine the tomato mixture, walnut halves, chives, lemon juice, vinegar, paprika, and remaining 1 tablespoon oil in a food processor. Process until smooth, about 1 minute.

SPICED SWEET POTATOES ON COUNTRY TOAST WITH BANANA PEPPERS AND CILANTRO

HANDS-ON: 15 MINUTES   TOTAL: **50 MINUTES**   SERVES **3**   **V**

This is a great starter to a winter meal, or, in any season, a perfect lunchtime sandwich. Pair it with a glass of chilled white wine.

15 pear tomatoes

2 poblano peppers, seeds removed and thinly sliced

2 tablespoons extra-virgin olive oil

1 pound Okinawan sweet potatoes or yams, peeled and cut lengthwise into ½-inch thick pieces

2 tablespoons roasted garlic oil

1 tablespoon sambal oelek

1 teaspoon ground cumin

1 teaspoon onion powder

1 teaspoon garlic powder

½ teaspoon ancho chile powder

Kosher salt and freshly ground black pepper, to taste

12 to 15 cilantro leaves, plus ½ cup leaves and tender stems

6 sweet banana peppers, thinly sliced

2 ½ tablespoons fresh lime juice and zest (about 2 limes)

¼ cup plain yogurt (not Greek-style)

6 slices whole-grain country bread

1 Preheat the oven to 400°F. Toss the tomatoes and sliced poblano peppers with the olive oil on a baking sheet; arrange in a single layer. Bake until tender, about 15 minutes. Set aside.

2 Toss the sweet potatoes, roasted garlic oil, sambal oelek, cumin, onion powder, garlic powder, chile powder, salt, and black pepper on a baking sheet and spread into an even layer; roast, flipping once, until cooked and browned, 20 minutes.

3 Mix the roasted tomatoes and poblano peppers, 12 to 15 cilantro leaves, banana peppers, 2 tablespoons of the lime juice, salt, and pepper in a bowl; set the dressing aside. Stir the yogurt and remaining ½ tablespoon lime juice in a bowl.

4 To assemble the sandwiches, layer 3 slices of the bread with the sweet potatoes, salsa, yogurt mixture, and the remaining ½ cup cilantro leaves. Top with the remaining slices of bread. Garnish with lime zest.

TIP

Okinawan sweet potatoes, also known as purple sweet potatoes, are high in antioxidants, potassium, and vitamin A, while low in carbs and calories. Try swapping in this heart-healthy and antiaging powerhouse for any recipes where you normally use yams.

MINI FALAFEL POCKET SANDWICHES

HANDS-ON: **28 MINUTES**   TOTAL: **1 HOUR, 28 MINUTES**   SERVES **4** (V)

Rich in plant protein and high in fiber, the falafel is a healthy, hearty replacement for red meat. The pita just makes it extra portable.

TAHINI-YOGURT SAUCE

⅓ cup plain yogurt (not Greek style)

2 tablespoons tahini (roasted sesame paste)

2 tablespoons cold water

1 tablespoon fresh lemon juice (from 1 lemon)

¼ teaspoon salt

¼ teaspoon freshly ground black pepper

FALAFEL

1 ⅓ cups boiling water

⅔ cup uncooked bulgur

2 garlic cloves

⅓ cup fresh parsley leaves

¼ cup fresh cilantro leaves

¾ teaspoon ground cumin

¼ teaspoon kosher salt

¼ teaspoon ground red pepper

1 (15-ounce) can chickpeas, drained and rinsed

1 large egg white

3 tablespoons olive oil

2 (6-inch) whole-wheat pitas, halved crosswise

1 cup chopped tomato

½ cup thinly sliced English cucumber

⅓ cup thinly sliced red onion

1 To prepare the Tahini-Yogurt Sauce: Combine the first 6 ingredients in a small bowl. Cover and chill until ready to serve.

2 To prepare the Falafel: Combine 1 ⅓ cups boiling water and the bulgur in a small bowl. Cover and let stand 25 to 30 minutes or until tender. Drain.

3 With the processor running, drop the garlic through the food chute, processing until minced. Add the bulgur, parsley, and next 6 ingredients, processing until smooth. Divide the mixture into 8 equal portions, shaping each into a ½-inch-thick patty. Place the patties on a baking sheet; cover and chill 30 minutes.

4 Heat 1 ½ tablespoons of the oil in a large nonstick skillet over medium-high. Add 4 patties; cook 3 minutes on each side or until golden brown. Repeat the procedure with the remaining 1 ½ tablespoons oil and 4 patties.

5 Spread 1 tablespoon Tahini-Yogurt Sauce inside each pita half. Fill each pita half with 2 patties, ¼ cup of the tomato, one-fourth of the cucumber slices, and one-fourth of the onion slices.

TIP

Sprinkle a teaspoon of spirulina on your falafel, if desired.

SWEET POTATO HASH BROWN OPEN-FACE SANDWICH WITH HAM AND CRANBERRY-DIJON BRUSSELS SLAW

HANDS-ON: **15 MINUTES**   TOTAL: **1 HOUR, 2 MINUTES**   SERVES **4** (DF)

Is it lunch or is it breakfast? Get ready because waffled hash browns are about to become your new favorite thing. Topping them with ham and veggies makes this a satisfying and complete meal.

2 medium-size sweet potatoes (about 20 ounces), peeled and grated

1 cup thinly sliced yellow onion

3 tablespoons brown rice flour

1 tablespoon coconut oil, melted, plus more for greasing waffle iron

1 large egg, lightly beaten

1 teaspoon kosher salt

3 tablespoons olive oil

2 tablespoons apple cider vinegar

2 teaspoons Dijon mustard

1 teaspoon pure maple syrup

8 ounces Brussels sprouts, shaved

⅓ cup dried cranberries

8 ounces nitrate-free reduced-sodium thinly sliced cooked ham

1 Preheat a waffle iron to HIGH. Combine the grated sweet potato, onion slices, flour, 1 tablespoon coconut oil, egg, and ½ teaspoon of the salt in a medium bowl. Grease the waffle iron with coconut oil, and place about 1 ½ cups of the sweet potato mixture in the center of the waffle iron, spreading the mixture to create a 6-inch square. Close the waffle iron, and cook until browned and tender, about 13 minutes. Remove the waffled sweet potato hash brown, and repeat the procedure to make 3 more hash browns.

2 Whisk together the olive oil, vinegar, mustard, maple syrup, and remaining ½ teaspoon salt in a medium bowl. Add the shaved Brussels sprouts; toss to coat. Let stand until the sprouts are tender, about 10 minutes. Fold in the cranberries.

3 Put 1 hash brown on each of 4 plates. Top each with 2 ounces ham slices and about ⅔ cup Brussels slaw.

WARM BACON, AVOCADO, AND COMTÉ ON TOASTED RUSTIC BREAD

HANDS-ON: **15 MINUTES**   TOTAL: **15 MINUTES**   SERVES **2**

Mmm. Warm avocado with thick-cut bacon is enough to make all of us happy, but adding the Comté puts the cherry on top. The texture of this world-famous cheese—French, of course, and closely related to Gruyère—can vary from silky smooth to almost as crystalline as a hard, aged Parmesan. The hint of lemon makes it come alive, and the egg just tops off the triumph of this dish.

- 4 hormone- and nitrate-free thick-cut bacon slices
- 4 thick rustic white bread slices, toasted and warm
- 2 tablespoons mayonnaise
- 4 (¼-inch-thick) heirloom tomato slices
- 1 ripe avocado, cut into slices
- 4 crisp baby romaine lettuce leaves, soaked in ice water and drained
- 2 teaspoons unsalted butter
- 2 large eggs
- 4 (½-ounce) Comté cheese slices
- 2 teaspoons lemon zest (from 1 lemon)

1 Place the bacon slices in a skillet over medium. Cook, turning occasionally, until crisp, about 8 minutes. Transfer to a plate lined with paper towels to drain.

2 Spread each of 2 toasted bread slices with 1 tablespoon mayonnaise. Layer each with 2 bacon slices, 2 tomato slices, half of the avocado slices, and 2 lettuce leaves.

3 Melt the butter in a nonstick skillet over medium. Add 1 egg, and cook until crisp around the edges, about 2 minutes per side. (The yolk should still be very runny.) Slide the egg onto the lettuce of 1 sandwich. Repeat with the remaining egg. Top each egg with 2 Comté slices, sprinkle with the zest, and cover with 1 toasted bread slice.

PEAR, BRIE, HAM TOASTS

HANDS-ON: **20 MINUTES**   TOTAL: **30 MINUTES**   MAKES: **12 HORS D'OEUVRE SERVINGS**

Ham and cheese is a combo that never goes out of style. This fancy toast version makes a quick lunch or filling snack.

6 slices whole-grain bread

2 tablespoons unsalted butter, melted

½ cup pear preserves or chutney

2 tablespoons grainy Dijon mustard

¼ teaspoon smoked paprika or cayenne

Kosher salt, to taste

8 ounces Brie, with rind, thinly sliced

4 ounces sliced serrano ham or prosciutto

½ red Bartlett pear, cored and thinly sliced

1 Preheat the oven to 350°F. Brush the bread with the butter and arrange it on a baking sheet. Toast in preheated oven until golden and crisp, turning each slice once, about 10 minutes.

2 Turn on the broiler. In a bowl, combine the pear preserves, mustard, paprika, and salt and spread on the bread. Top with the Brie, and broil until melted. Top with the ham and pear slices; cut into triangles and serve.

WARM HAM AND SPINACH ON RYE WITH GRUYÈRE

HANDS-ON: **15 MINUTES**   TOTAL: **25 MINUTES**   SERVES **4**

There are numerous variations on the iconic French croque-monsieur sandwich. Mine uses spinach, cucumbers, and Worcestershire.

8 slices rye bread

Olive oil for brushing

1 cucumber, thinly sliced

½ teaspoon tumeric

3 tablespoons cider vinegar

2 tablespoons olive oil

2 teaspoons coconut sugar

½ teaspoon red chile flakes

Kosher salt and black pepper, to taste

⅓ cup mayonnaise

1 teaspoon Worcestershire sauce

Small handful of spinach

1 pound boneless organic ham, thinly shaved

4 slices Gruyère cheese

1 Preheat the oven to 400°F. Brush the bread with the olive oil and arrange it on a baking sheet. Toast until golden and crisp.

2 Combine the cucumber, tumeric, vinegar, oil, coconut sugar, and red chile flakes. Season with salt and black pepper.

3 Combine the mayonnaise and Worcestershire sauce; mix well. Spread on the bread.

4 Divide the cucumber mixture and raw spinach among 4 of the bread slices. Add the ham and cheese and bake until the cheese is melted, about 5 minutes. Cover with the remaining bread.

CHICKEN MEATBALL BANH MI

HANDS-ON: 1 HOUR, 15 MINUTES   **TOTAL: 1 HOUR, 15 MINUTES**   SERVES **6**   **DF**

My version of the epic Vietnamese-French sandwich is all about texture, the balance between acidity and spiciness, and the crunch of the vegetables and the crusty bread.

PICKLED VEGETABLES

1 tablespoon bottled yuzu juice

½ cup unseasoned rice vinegar

¼ cup coconut sugar

1 teaspoon red chile flakes

1 teaspoon kosher salt

2 cups julienned cucumber

2 cups julienned carrots

2 cups julienned daikon

SPICY MAYONNAISE

1 ½ cups mayonnaise

½ teaspoon fish sauce

1 tablespoon minced red onion

6 tablespoons cilantro leaves, chopped

1 to 2 tablespoons hot chili sauce

1 tablespoon grated ginger

MEATBALLS

1 pound ground chicken

¼ cup chopped fresh basil

4 garlic cloves, minced

2 shallots, finely chopped

½ cup cilantro leaves, chopped, plus sprigs for garnish

4 green onions, finely chopped

1 tablespoon chopped fresh ginger

2 tablespoons fish sauce

1 tablespoon gochujang

2 tablespoons coconut sugar

2 teaspoons cornstarch

1 teaspoon kosher salt

1 teaspoon freshly ground black pepper

3 tablespoons duck fat

6 hero rolls or 6-inch baguettes

2 jalapeño chiles, sliced

1 To prepare the Pickled Vegetables: Combine the yuzu juice and vinegar in a bowl. Stir in the ¼ cup sugar, red chile flakes, and 1 teaspoon salt until dissolved. Add the julienned cucumber, carrots, and daikon. Cover with plastic wrap. Let the vegetables marinate at room temperature, about 1 hour, tossing occasionally.

2 To prepare the Spicy Mayonnaise: Combine the mayonnaise and next 5 ingredients in a small bowl. Cover and chill.

3 To prepare the Meatballs: Gently mix the ground chicken and next 12 ingredients in a large bowl. Using moistened hands, shape the mixture into 1 ½- to 1 ¾-inch meatballs.

4 Heat the duck fat in a skillet over medium-high. Working in batches, sauté the meatballs until cooked through, turning to brown on all sides. Keep warm.

5 Slice the rolls open lengthwise. Toast in the oven, if desired. Coat the insides of the rolls with the spicy mayonnaise. Divide the meatballs among the sandwiches. Top with the pickled vegetables, jalapeño slices, and cilantro sprigs.

TIP

Gochujang is a Korean chile paste. If you don't have it on hand, use Sriracha or another chile sauce.

DAIKON WRAPS WITH CUCUMBER, AVOCADO, AND SPROUTS

HANDS-ON: **30 MINUTES**   TOTAL: **30 MINUTES**   SERVES **4**   (GF) (DF)

Strips of daikon radish make for a fresh and pretty presentation. Use a cheese slicer or mandoline to cut thin strips the length of the radish. Each daikon strip should make two rolls.

½ small ripe avocado

¼ teaspoon fine sea salt

3 teaspoons fresh lime juice (from 1 lime)

1 medium or large daikon, cut lengthwise using a mandoline into 8 very thin slices

8 ounces smoked salmon, cut into 8 pieces

½ medium-size English cucumber, cut into 16 (2- x ½-inch) pieces

½ cup kale sprouts, broccoli sprouts, or alfalfa sprouts

2 tablespoons liquid aminos or soy sauce

1 tablespoon sambal oelek

2 teaspoons coconut sugar

2 teaspoons rice vinegar

1 Mash the avocado in a small bowl; stir in the salt and 1 teaspoon of the lime juice. Spread the avocado mixture on the daikon slices. At 1 short end of 1 daikon slice, place 1 piece of salmon, 2 cucumber pieces, and about 1 tablespoon of the sprouts. Roll the daikon slice over the filling, and continue rolling tightly to the other short end. Repeat the procedure to make 7 more wraps.

2 Stir together the liquid aminos, sambal oelek, coconut sugar, vinegar, and remaining 2 teaspoons lime juice in a small bowl until the sugar dissolves. Serve with the daikon wraps.

BANGING BOWLS: GRAINS AND SUSTAINABLE ALL-IN-ONE, ANYTIME, ANYWHERE MEALS

Did we really have to wait till the 21st century to figure out that it makes a lot of sense to put all sorts of different foods together in a bowl and call it—wait for it—a "bowl"? I guess it was worth the wait because bowls are trending big-time, and they are also obviously here to stay. About time, too.

In these recipes, you will find balanced, sustainable proteins and grains in wonderfully flavorful combinations to make delicious meals that satisfy your health requirements and your senses of sight, smell, and, above all, taste—all in a single bowl.

EASY CAULIFLOWER RICE
WITH ROASTED VEGETABLES
AND CHICKEN

HANDS-ON: **20 MINUTES**   TOTAL: **55 MINUTES**   SERVES **4**   (GF) (DF)

If you haven't embraced the cauliflower rice trend yet, this is your chance. Cauliflower adds fiber, vitamins, and potassium, while letting you cut carbs. Plus, this curry bowl is just delicious.

1 pound Brussels sprouts, trimmed, halved lengthwise

1 (8-ounce) package peeled baby carrots with tops, halved lengthwise

1 small red onion, halved, cut into ¾-inch wedges

¼ cup olive oil

¾ teaspoon kosher salt

½ teaspoon black pepper

1 rotisserie chicken

2 tablespoons finely chopped jarred preserved lemon

2 tablespoons finely chopped shallot

2 tablespoons apple cider vinegar

1 teaspoon coconut sugar

1 teaspoon Madras curry powder

1 head cauliflower (about 2 pounds), cut into florets

¼ cup chopped, roasted unsalted cashews

1 Preheat the oven to 425°F. Toss together the Brussels sprouts, carrots, onion, 1 tablespoon of the olive oil, ½ teaspoon of the salt, and ¼ teaspoon of the black pepper in a bowl. Spread the mixture in an even layer on a rimmed baking sheet. Bake in preheated oven until the vegetables are tender and caramelized, about 25 minutes.

2 Remove and discard the skin from the chicken. Remove the meat, and shred to equal about 2 cups. Whisk together the preserved lemon, shallot, vinegar, coconut sugar, curry powder, and 2 tablespoons of the olive oil in a small bowl. Toss the shredded chicken with 3 tablespoons of the dressing.

3 Pulse the florets in a food processor until the cauliflower is finely chopped and resembles uncooked rice or couscous. Heat the remaining 1 tablespoon olive oil in a large nonstick skillet over medium-high; add the cauliflower and remaining ¼ teaspoon each of salt and pepper, and cook, stirring once or twice, until just beginning to brown, about 8 minutes. Divide the cauliflower evenly among 4 bowls; top with the caramelized vegetables and chicken, and drizzle with the remaining dressing. Sprinkle with the cashews.

TIP

You can use cauliflower rice as an easy side that goes with anything you normally would serve with regular rice. One head of cauliflower gives you about 4 cups of "rice."

FRIED QUINOA WITH PICKLED COLLARD GREENS, AVOCADO, AND EGGS FOR DIPPING

HANDS-ON: **40 MINUTES**   TOTAL: **5 HOURS, 40 MINUTES**   SERVES **4**   Ⓥ ⒹⒻ

Fried rice has become an American staple. Healthwise, however, it's probably not the best thing for us. Fried quinoa is its flavorful and healthier cousin, especially alongside collard greens. You'll need four hours to chill the greens; I guarantee you it's worth it.

1 cup water

½ cup apple cider vinegar

3 tablespoons pure maple syrup

6 collard green leaves, cut into thin strips (about 3 cups)

2 cucumbers, peeled and diced (about 1 ½ cups)

2 cups low-sodium mushroom broth or vegetable broth

1 cup uncooked red quinoa, rinsed

⅓ cup drained pickled ginger, thinly sliced into ribbons

1 ½ teaspoons kosher salt

½ cup red wine vinegar

4 large eggs

2 tablespoons grapeseed or safflower oil

3 garlic cloves, thinly sliced (about 1 ½ tablespoons)

2 shallots, thinly sliced (about ¼ cup)

½ red onion, finely diced (about 1 cup)

6 cups loosely packed fresh arugula, torn

2 ripe avocados, halved, pits removed

1 tablespoon adobo seasoning

¼ teaspoon black pepper

1 Stir together 1 cup water, apple cider vinegar, and maple syrup in a saucepan over high, and bring to a boil. Remove the pan from the heat, and let cool 30 minutes. Place the maple syrup mixture in the refrigerator until chilled, about 1 hour. Pour the chilled maple syrup mixture over the collards and diced cucumbers in a large bowl; cover and chill at least 4 hours. (You can do this the day before.)

2 Meanwhile, bring the broth, quinoa, ginger, and 1 teaspoon of the salt to a boil in a medium saucepan over medium-high. Cover, reduce heat to low, and cook until the quinoa is tender, 8 to 10 minutes. Remove from the heat, and let stand, covered, 15 minutes; fluff with a fork.

3 Bring 2 inches of water to a boil in a large nonstick saucepan over medium-high; reduce the heat to low, and bring the water to a simmer. Stir in the red wine vinegar. Crack 1 egg into a small bowl, and gently slip into simmering water. Repeat with the remaining eggs, adding just as the whites of the eggs in the simmering water turn opaque, about 30 seconds. Cook the eggs until the whites are set but the yolks are still runny or until desired doneness, about 3 minutes. Using a slotted spoon, transfer the eggs to paper towels.

4 Heat the oil in a large skillet over medium-high. Add the garlic, shallots, and red onion, and cook, stirring often, 2 minutes. Add the cooked quinoa, and cook, stirring often, until the quinoa is nutty and aromatic, about 1 minute; stir in the arugula just until wilted.

5 Divide the quinoa-and-arugula mixture evenly among 4 serving bowls. Using the tip of a sharp knife, score the flesh of each avocado half into diamond shapes. Using a spoon, scoop out the avocado cubes from the shell, and divide evenly among the bowls. Top each with about ⅓ cup drained pickled collards-and-cucumber mixture and 1 poached egg. Sprinkle with the adobo seasoning, black pepper, and remaining ½ teaspoon salt.

WHITE BEANS AND SMOKED PAPRIKA CHICKEN WITH BLACK RICE

HANDS-ON: **40 MINUTES**   TOTAL: **40 MINUTES, PLUS 8 HOURS BRINING**   SERVES **4**   **GF** **DF**

Rice and beans together create the food staple that half the world relies on for basic nutrition. And on that foundation, some of the whole world's greatest-tasting dishes have been built. I've added smoked paprika chicken and a range of spices to create another one here.

1 (3-pound) whole chicken, brined (page 239)

5 tablespoons olive oil

1 ½ tablespoons smoked paprika

½ teaspoon fine sea salt

½ teaspoon black pepper

PEACH-AND-TOMATO TOSS

1 cup seeded and diced vine-ripened tomatoes

1 cup peeled and chopped fresh peaches

½ cup loosely packed fresh cilantro leaves, torn

⅓ cup loosely packed fresh basil leaves, torn

½ teaspoon lime zest, plus 2 tablespoons fresh lime juice (from 1 lime)

3 tablespoons finely chopped red onion

2 tablespoons grapeseed oil

½ teaspoon fine sea salt

¼ teaspoon black pepper

WHITE BEANS

2 tablespoons grapeseed oil

4 garlic cloves, smashed and finely chopped (about 1 ½ tablespoons)

⅓ cup finely chopped red bell pepper or red Fresno chile (much hotter)

1 shallot, finely diced (about 2 tablespoons)

1 tablespoon chopped peeled fresh ginger

2 tablespoons finely chopped red onion

3 cups low-sodium chicken broth

2 (15-ounce) cans white beans, drained and rinsed

1 ½ tablespoons chili powder

1 teaspoon ground turmeric

1 teaspoon ground coriander

¾ teaspoon cumin seeds

½ teaspoon fine sea salt

¼ teaspoon black pepper

4 cups cooked black rice or wild rice

1 teaspoon fine sea salt

¼ teaspoon black pepper

Lime wedges

1 Preheat the oven to 350°F. Pat the brined chicken dry with paper towels. Brush with 3 tablespoons of the olive oil; rub with the smoked paprika, and ½ teaspoon each of the sea salt and black pepper. Place the chicken in a lightly greased roasting pan, and bake in preheated oven 1 hour. Increase the oven temperature to 400°F, and bake until a meat thermometer inserted in thigh registers 165°F, about 15 minutes. Let the chicken stand until slightly cooled, about 20 minutes.

2 Remove the meat from the bones, and shred to equal about 3 cups. Toss together the chicken and remaining 2 tablespoons olive oil in a bowl, and set aside.

3 To prepare the Peach-and-Tomato Toss: Combine the tomatoes, peaches, torn cilantro, torn basil, lime zest, 1 tablespoon of the lime juice, 3 tablespoons finely chopped red onion, 2 tablespoons grapeseed oil, ½ teaspoon sea salt, and ¼ teaspoon black pepper in a bowl.

To prepare the White Beans: Heat 2 tablespoons grapeseed oil in a large skillet over medium; add the garlic, bell pepper, shallot, chopped ginger, and 2 tablespoons finely chopped red onion, and cook, stirring often, until the vegetables are translucent, aromatic, and soft, about 4 minutes. Whisk in the broth and white beans, and bring to a boil. Reduce the heat to medium, and simmer, stirring often and mashing the beans with the back of a wooden spoon until the mixture is slightly thickened, 6 to 8 minutes. Stir in the chili powder, turmeric, coriander, cumin seeds, ½ teaspoon sea salt, and ¼ teaspoon black pepper.

To prepare the bowls: Divide the rice evenly among 4 serving bowls; top with the bean mixture. Toss the chicken with the remaining 1 tablespoon lime juice (from Peach-and-Tomato Toss), 1 teaspoon sea salt, and ¼ teaspoon black pepper; top each bowl with about ¾ cup shredded chicken and about ½ cup of the Peach-and-Tomato Toss. Serve with lime wedges.

GLUTEN-FREE SHELLS AND CHEESE WITH PEAS

HANDS-ON: **10 MINUTES**   TOTAL: **35 MINUTES**   SERVES **6**   GF   V

Avoiding gluten doesn't have to mean mac and cheese is completely out of reach. This creamy version of the comfort-food favorite will keep your energy up on an active day. Check the label to ensure you are using gluten-free Dijon mustard.

1 (8-ounce) box gluten-free pasta shells

3 tablespoons unsalted butter

¼ cup brown rice flour

2 ½ cups unsweetened almond milk

4 ounces Gruyère cheese, shredded (about 1 cup)

1 ½ teaspoons Dijon mustard

1 teaspoon kosher salt

½ teaspoon black pepper

¼ teaspoon cayenne pepper

8 ounces extra-sharp Cheddar cheese, shredded (about 2 cups) or 12 ounces almond cheese (about 3 cups)

1 cup frozen peas

½ cup gluten-free panko (Japanese-style breadcrumbs)

1 ½ teaspoons fresh thyme leaves

1 Preheat the oven to 425°F.

2 Cook the pasta according to the package directions; drain.

3 Meanwhile, melt 2 tablespoons of the butter in a large saucepan over medium. Add the brown rice flour, and cook, whisking constantly, 1 minute. Gradually whisk in the almond milk. Bring to a boil, and cook, whisking often, until thickened, about 1 minute. Reduce the heat to low; whisk in the Gruyère cheese, mustard, salt, black pepper, cayenne pepper, and 1 ½ cups of the Cheddar cheese. Stir in the peas and cooked pasta. Spoon the mixture into a lightly greased 11- x 7-inch (2-quart) baking dish.

4 Microwave the remaining 1 tablespoon butter in a small microwave-safe bowl at HIGH until melted, about 30 seconds. Stir in the panko until combined. Stir in the thyme and remaining ½ cup Cheddar cheese; sprinkle over the mixture in the baking dish.

5 Bake in preheated oven until golden brown and bubbly, 15 to 20 minutes.

Gluten-free pasta tends to cook faster than other pasta. Check for doneness a few minutes before the package indicates.

WHITE FISH CURRY

HANDS-ON: **50 MINUTES**   TOTAL: **1 HOUR, 50 MINUTES**   SERVES **8**   **DF**

Sometimes, I just get a yen for a well-made curry, and nothing else will do. So I wanted to share my own curry recipe with all of you out there who get the same itch. Here's the answer—a white fish curry that, believe me, is simply kick-ass. Caution your guests not to eat the star anise or green cardamom pods as the heat of both is intense.

4 green cardamom pods

2 star anise pods

1 ½ teaspoons ground cinnamon

1 teaspoon ground turmeric

½ cup grapeseed oil

2 cups thinly sliced Vidalia onions

2 cups cubed red potatoes

4 garlic cloves, smashed and chopped

1 cup drained pickled ginger, thinly sliced into ribbons

½ teaspoon sambal oelek

4 kaffir lime leaves, bruised

½ tablespoon green curry paste

1 (15-ounce) can chickpeas, drained and rinsed

2 cups coconut milk

2 cups canned tomatoes, drained

½ cup rice vinegar

½ cup water

½ cup fresh mango juice

2 tablespoons fresh lime juice

2 tablespoons cumin seeds, toasted and ground

2 tablespoons white sesame seeds, toasted and ground

1 tablespoon fenugreek seeds, toasted and ground

1 teaspoon kosher salt

½ teaspoon black pepper

2 pounds cubed local white fish

1 Heat a large, heavy-bottomed Dutch oven or saucepan over medium-high. (Do not add oil.) Add the cardamom, star anise, cinnamon, and turmeric, and cook, stirring constantly, until toasted, about 60 seconds. Add the grapeseed oil to the Dutch oven, and stir until hot. Add the onions, potatoes, garlic, and pickled ginger, and cook, stirring often, just until the mixture begins to caramelize, 5 to 7 minutes. Stir in the sambal oelek, kaffir lime leaves, and green curry paste, and cook, stirring often, 1 minute.

2 Add the chickpeas, coconut milk, tomatoes, vinegar, ½ cup water, mango juice, lime juice, cumin seeds, white sesame seeds, fenugreek seeds, salt, and pepper. Reduce the heat to medium-low, and simmer, stirring occasionally, 1 hour. Gently fold in the fish, and cook over medium until the fish is opaque, about 6 minutes. Remove the cardamom pods and star anise pods, and serve immediately.

SPICED SHRIMP-AND-FARRO BOWL

HANDS-ON: **40 MINUTES**   TOTAL: **40 MINUTES**   SERVES **4**   DF

Said to have been the favorite food of Roman legions, farro is an ancient grain, grown at high altitude, that is rich in vitamins, fiber, and magnesium and way low in gluten. Its nutty-ish taste and its light texture add a touch of elegance to this rich, spicy bowl.

5 tablespoons olive oil

7 cups thinly sliced red onions

2 shallots, diced

1 (3-inch) cinnamon stick

1 ½ tablespoons sambal oelek, plus more for topping

1 teaspoon fine sea salt

½ teaspoon freshly ground pink peppercorns

12 ounces peeled and deveined large raw shrimp, cut into ¾-inch pieces

2 celery stalks, thinly sliced on a mandoline (about 1 ¼ cups)

6 garlic cloves, thinly sliced on a mandoline (about 3 tablespoons)

2 ½ tablespoons chopped peeled fresh ginger

2 tablespoons finely chopped fresh lemongrass

2 ½ cups cooked farro

2 tablespoons bottled yuzu juice

2 tablespoons rice vinegar

1 tablespoon tamari

2 teaspoons roasted garlic oil

4 large eggs

¼ cup chopped fresh cilantro

¼ cup chopped fresh basil

¼ cup chopped fresh mint

¼ cup chopped fresh flat-leaf parsley

1 Heat 3 tablespoons of the olive oil in a large skillet over medium. Add the sliced red onions, diced shallots, cinnamon stick, and 1 ½ tablespoons of the sambal oelek, and cook, stirring often, until the shallots and onions are lightly caramelized, 8 to 10 minutes. Sprinkle the mixture with the sea salt and ground peppercorns. Using a slotted spoon, remove the mixture from the skillet to a baking sheet lined with paper towels, and spread in an even layer. Discard the cinnamon stick.

2 Increase the heat to high; add the shrimp, celery, garlic, ginger, and lemongrass to the skillet, and cook, tossing the mixture until the shrimp are cooked through and turn pink, about 3 minutes. Remove the shrimp mixture from the skillet.

3 Heat 1 tablespoon of the olive oil in the skillet; add the farro, pressing against the bottom and sides of the skillet until a crust forms. Cook until the grains start to pop, about 1 minute. Toss the farro, and press again on the bottom and sides of the skillet. Cook until lightly toasted, about 4 minutes. Return the shrimp to the skillet; add the yuzu juice, vinegar, tamari, and roasted garlic oil, and cook, gently stirring until the liquid is absorbed, about 1 minute. Spoon about 1 ½ cups shrimp mixture into each of 4 serving bowls.

4 Heat the remaining 1 tablespoon olive oil in the skillet over medium-high. Crack the eggs into the skillet, and cook until the whites are set but the yolks are still runny, about 3 minutes. Top each bowl with 1 fried egg, ½ cup of the caramelized red onion mixture, and desired amount of sambal oelek. Toss together the cilantro, basil, mint, and parsley; sprinkle about ¼ cup herb mixture over each bowl.

SUNFLOWER, RAINBOW CHARD, AND MINT GRAIN BOWL WITH EGG

HANDS-ON: **1 HOUR, 30 MINUTES**   TOTAL: **1 HOUR, 30 MINUTES**   SERVES **4**   GF V DF

Sometimes, you need a detox—maybe a fresh start Sunday morning after a way-too-rich Saturday night—and this is the way to go. Hearty and homey, this recipe hits all the essentials of clean nutrition with flavor to burn. A high-tech, high-taste way to renew body and soul.

6 cups water

¾ teaspoon kosher salt

⅔ cup uncooked red quinoa, well rinsed

½ cup white vinegar

4 large eggs

1 bunch Swiss chard, thick ribs removed and leaves torn into large pieces

1 tablespoon roasted garlic oil

3 garlic cloves, very thinly sliced

4 organic sunflowers, petals removed and reserved

4 tablespoons finely chopped peeled fresh ginger

3 tablespoons rice wine vinegar

2 tablespoons tamari

1 shallot, very thinly sliced

¼ cup peanut oil

1 teaspoon sesame oil

2 cups cooked brown rice

1 ripe avocado, sliced

1 cup roughly chopped kimchi

½ cup loosely packed fresh mint leaves, cut into long, thin strips

⅓ cup sliced scallions

1 radish, thinly sliced on a mandoline and cut into thin strips

Sesame seeds

Crumbled nori

1 Bring 2 cups of the water and ½ teaspoon of the salt to a boil in a saucepan over medium-high; stir in the quinoa. Cover, reduce the heat to low, and simmer 15 minutes. Remove the pan from the heat, and let the quinoa stand, covered, 5 minutes. Fluff with a fork.

2 Bring ½ cup white vinegar and the remaining 4 cups water to a boil in a large saucepan. Using a slotted spoon, carefully lower the eggs into the boiling water, and cook 6 minutes. Drain and immediately transfer the eggs to a bowl of ice water to cool.

3 Bring about 1 to 1 ½ inches of water to a boil in a large saucepan fitted with a steamer basket. Arrange the chard in the basket. Cover and steam until tender, about 2 minutes.

4 Heat the roasted garlic oil in a skillet over medium-high; add the garlic, and cook, stirring often, 1 minute. Stir in the sunflower petals; remove the petal-garlic mixture from the skillet, and set aside.

5 Whisk together the ginger, rice vinegar, tamari, shallot, and remaining ¼ teaspoon of salt. Whisk in the peanut oil and sesame oil.

6 Spoon about ½ cup each of the cooked quinoa and rice into each of 4 bowls. Divide the chard evenly among the bowls, mounding on top of the quinoa mixture. Arrange the avocado slices around the chard. Peel the eggs, and cut in half; add two egg halves to each bowl. Sprinkle each bowl with the garlic sunflower petals, kimchi, mint, scallions, radish, sesame seeds, and crumbled nori. Drizzle the tamari dressing evenly over the mixture in the bowls.

4 FOOD FOR THE HUSTLE

There are days when there's little chance for a real meal, whether you're moving from place to place, appointment to appointment, or simply stuck in one place all day—at a workshop or seminar, or on an airplane. Days like that can really take it out of you, but you can periodically reboot if you put together one or more of these quick snacks to punctuate the day. The multifaceted aim is taste that can wake up your senses, nutrients that can boost your energy, and a bit of comfort to calm the commotion.

County*

"A Family Operated Farm Located in Historic Hunterdon County"

NET WEIGHT 1.5 LB.

No Additives

"A Fa

"A Family Operated Farm Located in Historic Hunterdon County"

NET WEIGHT 1 LB.

NET WEIGHT 2 LB.

COLD SOBA NOODLES WITH ROASTED TOMATO OIL, KALAMATA OLIVES, AND SHAVED PARMESAN CHEESE

HANDS-ON: **30 MINUTES**   TOTAL: **30 MINUTES**   SERVES **6**

Classic Asian meets classic Italian, providing a rainbow of flavors and textures to wake up nearly all your senses. Pleasantly sweet umami taste from the smooth buckwheat and tomatoes harmonizes with the Parmesan's bold texture and nutty flavor, the salty anchovies, and the stand-up shallots, garlic, basil, and thyme. Marco Polo would have cheered.

½ cup grape tomatoes

¾ teaspoon kosher salt

¼ teaspoon black pepper

6 tablespoons olive oil

1 pound uncooked dried soba noodles

2 tablespoons finely chopped shallot

4 garlic cloves, grated

3 anchovies, chopped

1 ½ cups pitted kalamata olives, chopped

3 tablespoons fresh thyme leaves

3 tablespoons balsamic vinegar

3 tablespoons water

⅔ ounce shaved Parmesan cheese (about ⅓ cup)

¼ cup torn fresh basil

1 Preheat the broiler with the oven rack 6 inches from the heat. Place the tomatoes on a rimmed baking sheet. Broil until just popped and browned, about 5 minutes.

2 Process the broiled tomatoes, salt, pepper, and 4 tablespoons of the oil in a food processor until smooth.

3 Cook the soba noodles according to the package directions for al dente. Drain and rinse in cold water. Transfer to a bowl.

4 Heat the remaining 2 tablespoons olive oil in a large skillet over medium-high. Add the shallot, garlic, and anchovies; cook until fragrant and the shallot is translucent, 4 to 6 minutes. Add the olives, thyme, vinegar, 3 tablespoons water, and 2 tablespoons of the broiled tomato oil; cook until slightly reduced, about 3 minutes.

5 Add the remaining broiled tomato oil to the cooked soba noodles; toss to coat. Divide the noodle mixture among 6 bowls. Top each with about ¼ cup olive mixture. Top with the Parmesan and basil.

SAVORY CORN CAKE FRITTERS

HANDS-ON: **40 MINUTES**   TOTAL: **40 MINUTES**   SERVES **12**   (GF) (V)

Happily, you can find corn fritters all over the world, but on a recent surfing visit to Bali, I got to taste the Indonesian version—lighter and cleaner than just about any other. It inspired me to create my own take on that exotic version of a universal favorite.

1 cup (about 5.13 ounces) gluten-free all-purpose baking flour

½ cup (about 2.88 ounces) fine cornmeal

¼ cup (about 1.63 ounces) chickpea flour

1 tablespoon Old Bay seasoning

1 tablespoon fine sea salt

½ tablespoon baking powder

½ cup coconut sugar

3 tablespoons unsalted butter

1 large egg

1 tablespoon pure maple syrup

½ cup coconut milk or any nut milk

1 cup fresh corn kernels (from 2 ears)

Grapeseed oil, or a blend of grapeseed and olive oil

Tomato Sofrito (page 236)

1 Combine the all-purpose flour, cornmeal, chickpea flour, Old Bay, salt, and baking powder. Stir once.

2 Beat the coconut sugar and butter with an electric mixer at high speed until well blended. Add the egg and maple syrup; beat to combine. Add the flour mixture and milk; beat to combine. Stir in the corn.

3 Heat the oil in a deep fryer to 340°F. Using a 2-ounce ice-cream scoop, gently drop the batter into the hot oil. Fry until golden brown, 3 to 4 minutes. Using tongs, transfer the fritters to a plate lined with paper towels.

4 Serve the fritters with the Tomato Sofrito. Best way to eat them: cut a fritter in half, and dollop the sofrito on top.

MISO-PEANUT KALE CHIPS

HANDS-ON: **30 MINUTES**   TOTAL: **2 HOURS**   SERVES **8**   DF

You already know that kale chips are an amazing super healthy alternative to potato chips. The peanut butter and miso give these crispy chips an extra salty-sweet flavor boost.

½ cup natural unsweetened peanut butter (or make your own, page 234)

2 tablespoons warm water

1 tablespoon white miso

1 tablespoon nutritional yeast

2 teaspoons rice vinegar

2 teaspoons reduced-sodium soy sauce or tamari

1 teaspoon ground ginger

¼ teaspoon Sriracha chili sauce

1 scallion, chopped

2 garlic cloves, roughly chopped

1 pound curly kale, stems removed, torn into bite-size pieces

1 Preheat the oven to 200°F. Process the peanut butter, 2 tablespoons warm water, miso, yeast, vinegar, soy sauce, ginger, chili sauce, scallion, and garlic in a food processor until smooth.

2 Grease 3 large wire cooling racks with cooking spray or olive oil; place in rimmed baking sheets.

3 Toss the kale with the peanut butter mixture, rubbing the mixture into each leaf. Divide the kale among the prepared baking sheets, and spread into an even layer on each. Bake in preheated oven until the leaves are crispy, about 1 hour and 30 minutes.

SAM'S 6 TIPS FOR POWERING UP AND STAYING ENERGIZED

1 KILL THE SNOOZE BUTTON.

It's not your friend. It gives your body all kinds of mixed messages: Okay, sleep for three more minutes. Okay, get up. Okay, three more. And so on, as you spiral downward into total procrastination. Instead, whatever alarm you use, when it goes off, wake up and climb out of bed. My "alarm" is the natural sunlight that pours into my window in the morning, but whatever method you use, get up and get going.

2 EXERCISE FOR 20 MINUTES.

Yup, start charging up for the day by jumping around or lifting weights or running in place or dancing your ass off or dropping down for 20 pushups—whatever it takes to wake up your muscles, your organs, your mind, and your senses.

3 SNACK & DRINK WHEN NEEDED.

I carry my own energy bars (pages 118-123) and when I feel like I'm flagging just a bit, I'll bite into one. New York is also filled with places that mix up all kinds of vegetable and fruit smoothies and juices. Think about carrying a thermos of your favorite homemade smoothies or juice-ade (pages 34-39).

4 MEDITATE.

Like Oprah Winfrey, like the entire population of Fairfield, Iowa, like millions of people all over the world throughout much of history, I do Transcendental Meditation twice a day—20 minutes in the morning, 20 in the afternoon. And it has changed my life. In the stillness I am able to achieve, I find peace and calm, but also get recharged with amazing energy.

5 DON'T EAT TOO LATE.

Make sure you have dinner at least four hours before you go to sleep—certainly no later than 10pm. And to ensure a better sleep, keep that last meal lower in carbs and focused on vegetables and protein.

6 STRETCH BEFORE SLEEP.

I give myself a whole-body stretch when I get into bed: toes pointed at the bottom of the bed, neck supported and elongated, limbs as extended as I can get them. I try to empty my mind of whatever it's hanging onto, and I fill my lungs with air, hold it for a second or two, then exhale slowly. I'm practically asleep by the end of the stretch, and it's a sleep that lets me wake up ready to go.

CINNAMON-and-COCONUT CHICKPEAS

HANDS-ON: **10 MINUTES**   TOTAL: **1 HOUR, 40 MINUTES**   SERVES **4**   GF DF VG

Here's a great energy stabilizer for when you're on the go. The flavor is at once savory and sweet, but also mild. In short, the taste is awesome and the effect is balance in all things.

- 2 (14-ounce) cans chickpeas, drained and rinsed, patted dry with paper towels
- 2 teaspoons fine sea salt
- 2 teaspoons ground cinnamon
- 2 teaspoons ground cumin
- 1 teaspoon ground turmeric
- 1 teaspoon ground coriander
- ½ teaspoon red chile flakes
- 3 tablespoons unrefined coconut oil, melted
- 2 tablespoons ground unsweetened shredded coconut
- 1 ½ tablespoons lime zest

1 Preheat the oven to 325°F. Stir together the chickpeas, salt, cinnamon, cumin, turmeric, coriander, red chile flakes, melted coconut oil, and ground coconut in a large bowl. Spread on a rimmed baking sheet.

2 Bake in preheated oven until the chickpeas are crispy, about 1 hour and 30 minutes. Toss with the lime zest.

NO-BAKE TROPICAL ALMOND BUTTER BARS

HANDS-ON: **5 MINUTES**   TOTAL: **20 MINUTES**   SERVES **12**   (GF) (DF) (V)

Toasted oats add a nutty flavor to these easy-to-make bars. To toast the oats, coconut, and nuts, spread them in a thin layer on a baking sheet and bake in a 350°F oven for about 8 minutes.

12 pitted Medjool dates

1 ¼ cups uncooked regular rolled oats, toasted

½ cup unsweetened flaked coconut, toasted

½ cup chopped macadamia nuts, toasted

½ cup chopped dried pineapple

¼ cup unsweetened almond butter

¼ cup raw honey

2 tablespoons refined coconut oil

¼ teaspoon kosher salt

1 Line the bottom and sides of an 8-inch square baking dish with parchment paper, allowing a few excess inches of parchment to extend past the sides of the dish.

2 Process the dates in a food processor until finely chopped and the dates begin to form a ball. Transfer to a medium bowl; add the oats, coconut, macadamia nuts, and pineapple. Stir to combine.

3 Combine the almond butter, honey, coconut oil, and salt in a small saucepan over medium. Cook, stirring often, until smooth, about 2 minutes. Pour over the date mixture in bowl; stir until well blended. Spoon the mixture into the prepared baking dish. Top with a piece of plastic wrap, and press onto the surface of the mixture. Freeze until firm, about 15 minutes.

4 Using parchment, remove the frozen mixture from the baking dish. Cut into 12 bars.

ALL THE WAY UP ENERGY BARS

HANDS-ON: **20 MINUTES**   TOTAL: **30 MINUTES, PLUS COOLING TIME**   SERVES **16**   Ⓥ

This is one of my go-to energy bars, just the thing for late morning or afternoon when running around or doing too much has me flagging. It's a quick hit of concentrated nutrients—and a sweet, tasty comfort as well.

2 cups quinoa flakes (7 ounces)

1 cup sliced unblanched almonds

½ cup roasted, salted sunflower seeds

½ cup wheat germ (2 ounces)

2 tablespoons chia seeds

2 tablespoons protein powder

¼ cup goji berries

½ cup golden raisins

½ cup dried cherries

2 ounces (¼ cup) unsalted butter, plus more for the pan

½ cup plus 2 tablespoons coconut sugar

½ cup plus 2 tablespoons agave syrup

1 ½ teaspoons pure vanilla extract

½ teaspoon kosher salt

1 Preheat the oven to 350°F. On a sturdy, rimmed baking sheet, combine the quinoa flakes and almond. Toast in the center of the oven until golden and fragrant, about 10 minutes. Transfer the mixture to a large bowl and stir in the sunflower seeds, wheat germ, chia seeds, protein powder, goji berries, raisins, and dried cherries. Line the pan with parchment paper and lightly butter the paper.

2 In a medium saucepan, combine the 2 ounces butter with the coconut sugar and agave and bring to a boil. Cook over medium, stirring, until the sugar is just dissolved, about 2 minutes. Add the vanilla and salt. Pour the mixture into the bowl and stir until completely combined. Scrape the mixture onto the parchment and form it into a 6- x 12-inch rectangle, pressing it lightly to compact. Use a straightedge to evenly press the sides. Bake in the center of the preheated oven for 10 minutes, until very lightly browned. Cool slightly, then refrigerate until firm, about 20 minutes. Cut into 16 bars.

QUINOA-CHIA ENERGY BARS

HANDS-ON: **25 MINUTES**   TOTAL: **1 HOUR**   SERVES **16**   Ⓥ ⒹⒻ

Loaded with fiber, omega-3s, protein, carbs, and antioxidants, chia seeds paired with energy-revving quinoa make these bars perfect to keep you going. If you are sensitive to gluten, make sure to use gluten-free quinoa flakes.

⅔ cup apple juice

8 pitted Medjool dates, roughly chopped

3 tablespoons raw honey

1 ½ teaspoons pure vanilla extract

¼ cup chia seeds

1 teaspoon ground cinnamon

¾ teaspoon kosher salt

¼ cup unrefined coconut oil

1 ½ cups uncooked quinoa flakes

1 cup whole natural almonds, chopped

½ cup roasted hazelnuts, skins removed, chopped

⅔ cup dried cherries

⅔ cup chopped dried apricots

1 Preheat the oven to 350°F. Line the bottom and sides of a 13- x 9-inch baking dish with parchment paper, allowing a few excess inches of parchment to extend past the sides of the dish.

2 Bring the apple juice to a simmer in a small saucepan over medium-high. Remove from the heat; add the dates. Let stand until the dates are slightly softened, about 10 minutes. Transfer the mixture to a blender or food processor; add the honey and vanilla, and process until smooth. Transfer to a medium bowl; stir in the chia seeds, cinnamon, and salt. Let stand until the chia thickens slightly, about 10 minutes.

3 Melt the coconut oil in a large skillet over medium. Add the quinoa flakes, almonds, and hazelnuts. Cook, stirring often, until lightly toasted and fragrant, 3 to 4 minutes. Remove from the heat; cool slightly. Add the quinoa flake mixture, cherries, and apricots to the date mixture in the bowl; stir until well blended. Spoon the mixture into the prepared baking dish, and press into an even layer.

4 Bake in preheated oven until golden brown, about 35 minutes. Cool completely in the dish on a wire rack, about 1 hour. Using the parchment, lift the mixture out of the pan. Cut into 16 bars.

CELERY ROOT-AND-JICAMA SLAW

HANDS-ON: **20 MINUTES**   TOTAL: **20 MINUTES**   SERVES **8**   **GF**

"Traditional" coleslaw is typically made with tons of mayonnaise and wilting cabbage. Not my "modern" coleslaw. Fresh ingredients and real oil are the basis here. And while my Southern roots might suggest using sugar for sweetness—that's the way we do it below the Mason-Dixon Line—the jicama is the sweet spot here, along with an al dente crunchiness that makes your mouth wake up and take notice.

- ½ cup Brussels sprouts, trimmed, cores removed, and thinly sliced
- ½ cup roasted hazelnuts, roughly chopped
- 2 ounces Parmesan cheese, grated (about ½ cup)
- ⅓ cup loosely packed fresh flat-leaf parsley leaves
- ⅓ cup roughly chopped green olives
- ¼ cup extra-virgin olive oil
- ¼ cup fresh lemon juice (about 2 lemons)
- 3 tablespoons toasted pine nuts
- 2 tablespoons red wine vinegar
- ½ teaspoon kosher salt
- ½ teaspoon black pepper
- 3 celery stalks, diced
- 1 large celery root, peeled and sliced into matchsticks
- 1 small jicama, peeled, cut in half lengthwise, and sliced into matchsticks

Toss together all ingredients in a large bowl.

FLATBREAD WITH PESTO, MOZZARELLA, TOMATO, AND ARUGULA

HANDS-ON: **8 MINUTES** · TOTAL: **31 MINUTES** · SERVES **4** Ⓥ

This simple flatbread is loaded with fresh vegetable toppings.

2 cups halved grape tomatoes

1 tablespoon olive oil

4 (2-ounce) multigrain flatbreads

¼ cup pesto

4 ounces fresh mozzarella, shredded

4 cups loosely packed baby arugula leaves

⅛ teaspoon red chile flakes, optional

1 Preheat the oven to 400°F.

2 Combine the grape tomatoes and 1 teaspoon of the olive oil, tossing to coat. Place the tomatoes in a single layer on a rimmed baking pan. Bake in the preheated oven for 10 minutes or until softened. Reduce the oven temperature to 375°F.

3 Place the flatbreads on 2 baking sheets. Bake at 375°F for 5 minutes or until beginning to crisp. Spread 1 tablespoon pesto on each flatbread. Sprinkle each with ¼ cup mozzarella cheese and ½ cup roasted tomatoes. Bake at 375°F for 8 minutes or until the cheese is melted and bubbly.

4 While the flatbreads bake, combine the arugula and remaining 2 teaspoons olive oil, tossing well. Top the flatbreads evenly with arugula. Sprinkle with the red chile flakes, if desired.

WARM CAMEMBERT CHEESE

HANDS-ON: **15 MINUTES**   TOTAL: **15 MINUTES**   SERVES **6 TO 8**   Ⓥ

Camembert is the classic soft, creamy French cheese, and this recipe wraps it up in a unique flavor profile that features pungent and sweet, cool and real hot. It's a crowd-pleaser that works just as well as a snack on a crisp autumn day as it would as an accompaniment to an indulgent Mother's Day brunch.

1 tablespoon olive oil

⅓ cup very thinly sliced red onion

8 ounces fresh strawberries, quartered

½ cup Pinot Grigio or similar white wine

¼ cup raw honey

1 teaspoon Sriracha chili sauce

1 (14-ounce) Camembert or Brie cheese round

2 teaspoons finely chopped fresh chives

⅛ teaspoon sea salt

1 baguette, thinly sliced and toasted, or gluten-free toast points

1 Preheat the oven to 325°F. Heat the oil in a medium saucepan over medium-low. Add the onion, and cook, stirring often, until translucent and fragrant, about 3 minutes. Add the strawberries, and cook until the berries are tender and soft, 4 to 6 minutes. Add the wine, honey, and Sriracha; cook, stirring often, until thickened, 8 to 10 minutes.

2 Place the cheese on a parchment paper-lined baking sheet (or baking sheet lined with Silpat), and bake in preheated oven until warm, 3 to 5 minutes.

3 Place the warm cheese round on a serving platter; top with the warm strawberry sauce. Sprinkle with the chives and salt, and serve with the toasted baguette slices.

PLANTAIN CHIPS

HANDS ON: **6 MINUTES**   TOTAL: **12 MINUTES**   SERVES **4**   GF DF VG

Crunchy and slightly sweet, plantain chips are a great, gluten-free snack. Use a mandoline to get nice, thin slices.

¼ cup coconut oil

2 medium plantains, peeled and cut into ¼-inch diagonal slices (about 2 cups)

¼ teaspoon kosher salt

⅛ teaspoon ground red pepper

Heat a large nonstick skillet over medium heat. Add the oil to the skillet; swirl to coat. Add the plantain slices; cook 3 minutes on each side or until browned. Sprinkle the salt and pepper over the chips.

TIP

Store these chips in an airtight container at room temperature for up to 3 days.

WHITE BEAN GUACAMOLE

HANDS-ON: **15 MINUTES**   TOTAL: **15 MINUTES**   SERVES **6**   GF DF VG

If you think guacamole is strictly a summer dish for cocktails outside, and bean dishes are exclusively for hearty suppers in the dead of winter, think again. This white bean guacamole is both a great dish for holiday parties when the days are short and a solid nibbler for summer evenings that go on and on and on.

1 ripe avocado, diced (about 1 cup)

1 tablespoon sambal oelek

1 garlic clove, grated using a Microplane grater

¼ cup extra-virgin olive oil

1 tablespoon lime zest, plus 3 ½ tablespoons fresh juice (about 3 limes)

1 ½ cups cooked fresh white beans

1 cup diced beefsteak or heirloom tomatoes

2 tablespoons finely chopped red onion

¼ cup thinly sliced fresh cilantro

Tortilla chips or fruit and vegetable crudités, for serving

Combine the avocado, sambal oelek, garlic, oil, zest, juice, and 1 cup of the beans in a bowl; mash thoroughly. Gently fold in the tomatoes, onion, and remaining ½ cup beans. Sprinkle with the cilantro. Serve with the warm tortilla chips, crudités of fruit like apple or pear, or the usual vegetables.

TIP

To warm tortilla chips, spread on a baking sheet and bake at 350°F until warm, about 5 minutes.

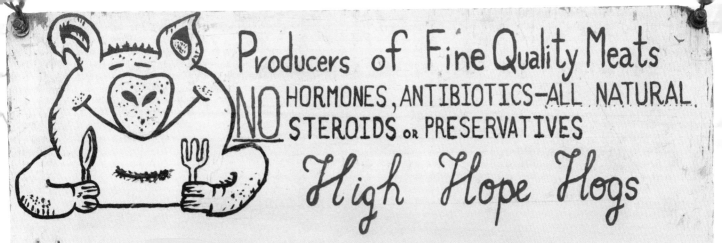

Producers of Fine Quality Meats
NO HORMONES, ANTIBIOTICS—ALL NATURAL. NO STEROIDS or PRESERVATIVES

High Hope Hogs

PROTEINS ON THE GROUND AND OUT OF THE SURF

I've long been involved with Seafood Watch (www.seafoodwatch.org), the Monterey Bay Aquarium's outreach to the food industry, including chefs like me, and to consumers to ensure healthy oceans and a sustainable supply of clean seafood. I'm similarly committed to humane and sustainable practices in the farming of animals for healthy animal products—organic, antibiotic-free, hormone-free.

Is this professional self-interest? You bet. Choosing ingredients with care, making sure that they can be responsibly replenished, means the long-term survival of a diversified food system, without which we won't need any chefs—or recipes like the ones that follow.

There's another reason, too: healthy fish and animal products create healthy humans. As someone who has to fight hard for good health, I know that counts big-time. Making good food choices is vital to our well-being and that of our Mother Earth. That's why it is so important to go the extra mile and, yes, pay the extra dollar for food that is cleanly and sustainably produced.

NO HORMONES LIVER NO ANTIBIOTICS NO STEROIDS

SMOKED PORK CHOPS "READY TO EAT"

"NEW YORK'S BEST SCRAPPLE BY THE "NEW YORK PRESS"

SMOKED HAM STEAKS "FULLY COOKED, READY TO EAT"

LEAF LARD

Yes we

Homemade All Natural *Applesauce* $4.50 pint Made only from pure Fresh Apples Nothing Else Added

ered Lard
n Chunks
d Hocks
vailable!
b.

Hams
& Boneless

LOOK inside and select your cuts of Pennsylvania Dutch Quality Natural Meats Featuring NO PRESERVATIVE Meats from our own Grain-fed Animals!

Pork

CHICKEN STICKS WITH ZUCCHINI AND APPLES

HANDS-ON: **30 MINUTES**   TOTAL: **50 MINUTES**   SERVES **4**   **DF**

This is a great appetizer for autumn—fresh and simple and vegetable-based with the distinctive flavors of fall. Try it with a seasonal beer, like an artisanal pumpkin ale, or with an apple cider, fermented or not.

4 boneless, skinless chicken thighs, cut into bite-size pieces

1 Granny Smith apple, cut into ½-inch cubes

1 green zucchini, cut into ½-inch cubes

1 yellow zucchini, cut into ½-inch cubes

½ cup ½-inch red onion pieces

8 wooden skewers

½ cup chopped fresh basil

⅓ cup rice vinegar

2 tablespoons grapeseed oil

1 ½ tablespoons Dijon mustard

2 garlic cloves, smashed and chopped

1 teaspoon kosher salt

¼ teaspoon black pepper

1 Preheat grill to medium (about 400°F). Thread the chicken, apple, green zucchini, yellow zucchini, and onion alternately onto 8 skewers.

2 Stir together the basil, rice vinegar, oil, mustard, garlic, salt, and pepper in a small bowl. Brush the mixture over the chicken-vegetable skewers. Grill, covered, turning occasionally, until the chicken is done, 12 to 14 minutes. Remove from the heat, and let stand 5 minutes.

SCALLOP-AND-CHICKEN SHUMAI

HANDS-ON: **1 HOUR, 30 MINUTES**   TOTAL: **1 HOUR, 30 MINUTES**   SERVES **12**   **DF**

I love Chinese dim sum and the delicate, beautiful dumplings known as shumai. If you think they're filled only with pork and scallions, you've got another think coming. Shumai varieties are as numerous as China's provinces, and now I'm adding my version.

FILLING

- ¾ pound sea scallops, drained and cut into ¼-inch pieces
- ½ pound ground chicken thighs
- 2 tablespoons finely chopped fresh lemongrass
- 2 tablespoons chopped peeled fresh ginger
- 1 tablespoon fresh lemon juice
- 1 tablespoon tamari or soy sauce
- 1 tablespoon red wine vinegar
- 2 teaspoons cornstarch
- 1 ½ teaspoons sesame oil
- ¼ teaspoon fine sea salt
- ¼ teaspoon ground white pepper
- 3 garlic cloves, chopped
- 2 large egg whites
- 1 scallion, minced

SHUMAI

- 2 large eggs
- 1 tablespoon almond milk
- 1 (10-ounce) package small round dumpling or wonton wrappers (wrappers should be about 3-inch rounds)

ADDITIONAL INGREDIENTS

- 1 tablespoon olive oil
- 4 to 5 romaine lettuce leaves
- 2 tablespoons minced fresh chives

1 To prepare the Filling: Pulse all of the filling ingredients in a food processor until almost smooth but not totally pureed.

2 To prepare the Shumai: Whisk together the eggs and almond milk in a small bowl. Working with 1 wrapper at a time, hold the wrapper in your palm and brush a small amount of the egg mixture on the outer edge of the wrapper. Place about 1 tablespoon of the filling in the center of the wrapper and gather up and pleat the edges all around the filling to form an open cup, gently squeezing the side and bottom of the wrapper so it adheres to the filling (you can gently tap the shumai on a work surface to flatten the bottom). Repeat with the remaining filling and wrappers. Cover the filled shumai with a damp paper towel to keep them from drying out before cooking.

3 Lightly brush the olive oil on the bottom of a bamboo steamer. (If you don't have a bamboo steamer, you can use a steamer pot.) Line with the romaine leaves. Working in batches, place the shumai in the steamer. (Make sure the shumai do not touch.)

4 Bring 1 to 2 inches of water to a boil over medium in a saucepan with sides high enough to hold the steamer without causing the water to overflow. Place the steamer inside the saucepan of boiling water; cover with the steamer lid. Cook until the filling is cooked through, 10 to 12 minutes. Remove the cooked shumai to a plate, and cover with damp paper towels to keep moist and warm. Repeat with the remaining shumai. Garnish with the chives.

TIP

You can serve it with a dipping sauce made from tamari, rice vinegar, and chile sauce.

JERK CHICKEN AND PINEAPPLE OVER GREENS AND CUKES

HANDS-ON: **30 MINUTES**   TOTAL: **30 MINUTES, PLUS 8 HOURS CHILLING**   SERVES **4**   **GF**   **DF**

My friend and manager, Joel Menzin, represents Toots and the Maytals, one of the greatest musical acts of all-time and major figures in the history of reggae. I wanted to show these guys that I could jerk chicken. This is the result.

4 tablespoons Chili Vinegar (or make your own, page 235)

2 Scotch bonnet or serrano chiles, seeds removed, chopped

3 tablespoons finely chopped pickled ginger

3 tablespoons pure maple syrup

2 tablespoons sesame oil

4 garlic cloves, finely chopped

1 teaspoon Chinese five-spice powder

¼ teaspoon ground nutmeg

¼ teaspoon ground cinnamon

1 ½ pounds boneless, skinless chicken thighs, cut into thin strips

3 tablespoons roasted garlic-infused olive oil

2 cups chopped fresh pineapple

½ cup chopped scallions

1 teaspoon kosher salt

1 teaspoon black pepper

1 cup diced cucumber, seeds removed

5 ounces fresh greens (such as arugula, bok choy, romaine lettuce, or your favorite seasonal locally grown greens)

½ cup loosely packed fresh mint leaves

1 Combine the chili vinegar, chiles, ginger, maple syrup, sesame oil, garlic, Chinese five-spice, nutmeg, and cinnamon in a glass baking dish. Add the chicken, and toss to coat. Cover and chill 8 hours or overnight.

2 Preheat the oven to 375°F. Drain the chicken well; discard the marinade. Heat the roasted garlic oil in a large nonstick ovenproof skillet over medium-high. Add the chicken, and cook, stirring occasionally, until browned, about 5 minutes. Transfer the chicken to a plate. Add the pineapple and scallions to the skillet; cook until just beginning to soften, about 2 minutes. Remove from the heat. Return the chicken to the skillet, and sprinkle with ½ teaspoon each salt and pepper. Stir to combine. Transfer to the oven, and bake until the chicken is cooked through, about 5 minutes.

3 Toss together the cucumber, greens, mint, and remaining ½ teaspoon each salt and pepper. Divide among 4 plates. Top with the chicken mixture.

PROTEINS ON THE GROUND AND OUT OF THE SURF

SKILLET-ROASTED CHICKEN LEGS WITH MEYER LEMON AND PICHOLINE OLIVES

HANDS-ON: **10 MINUTES**   TOTAL: **35 MINUTES**   SERVES **2**   GF DF

Bold spices, briny olives, and bright citrus elevate this flavorful chicken dish into an everyday superstar.

- ¾ teaspoon fine sea salt
- ¾ teaspoon ground cumin
- ½ teaspoon adobo seasoning
- ¼ teaspoon ground cinnamon
- ¼ teaspoon ground coriander
- 2 (1-pound) chicken leg quarters
- 1 medium-size yellow onion, sliced
- 1 Meyer lemon, cut into 8 wedges
- 1 large garlic clove, sliced
- 2 shallots, sliced
- ½ cup picholine olives, pits removed
- 2 tablespoons torn fresh flat-leaf parsley
- 1 tablespoon torn fresh cilantro

1 Preheat the oven to 425°F. Combine the salt, cumin, adobo seasoning, cinnamon, and coriander in a small bowl; rub all over the chicken leg quarters.

2 Heat a 9-inch cast-iron skillet over medium-high. Add the chicken, skin side down, and cook until well browned, 4 to 5 minutes. Turn the chicken, and cook 2 minutes. Remove the chicken to a plate. Add the onion, lemon, garlic, and shallots to the skillet; cook, stirring occasionally, until the onion is softened and the lemon is beginning to brown, about 4 minutes. Remove from the heat. Stir in the olives, and nestle the chicken, skin side up, in the onion mixture.

3 Bake in preheated oven until a meat thermometer inserted into thickest portion registers 165°F, about 25 minutes. Serve the chicken with the onion mixture and pan juices. Sprinkle the servings with the parsley and cilantro.

SWEET AND SPICY PORK

HANDS-ON: **30 MINUTES**   TOTAL: **30 MINUTES, PLUS 7 HOURS CHILLING**   SERVES **4**   GF DF

Here is an anytime, any-way-you-like-it, all-in-one meal—well-balanced, solid, sustaining, flavorful. Eat it like a taco in layers of rice and pork, or put it in a rice bowl with fresh lettuce and herbs, or make up your own way of enjoying it.

1 ½ pounds pork loin, cut into ¼-inch-thick slices

1 Fuji apple, grated (about 1 cup)

3 garlic cloves, grated on a Microplane grater

1 shallot, finely diced

1 jalapeño chile, seeds removed, finely chopped

2 tablespoons finely chopped peeled fresh ginger

2 tablespoons date sugar or coconut sugar

2 tablespoons sesame oil

2 tablespoons gluten-free tamari

1 tablespoon finely chopped lemongrass

1 tablespoon red wine vinegar

1 teaspoon ground cinnamon

1 teaspoon ground cumin

1 English cucumber, seeds removed, cut into half-moons

2 tablespoons coconut oil

1 teaspoon kosher salt

½ teaspoon black pepper

½ cup thinly sliced scallions

½ cup loosely packed cilantro leaves

2 tablespoons thinly sliced radishes (about 3 radishes)

Coconut Rice (recipe follows)

12 Bibb lettuce leaves

1 Stir together the pork, apple, garlic, shallot, jalapeño, ginger, date sugar, sesame oil, tamari, lemongrass, vinegar, cinnamon, cumin, and half of the cucumber slices in a bowl. Transfer the mixture to a 1-gallon zip-top plastic freezer bag. (I like to double-bag, just in case a tear or hole develops.) Seal the bag, and massage the ingredients in the bag until well combined. Chill 7 to 24 hours.

2 Heat 1 tablespoon of the coconut oil in a large cast-iron skillet over medium. Remove the pork from the marinade; discard the marinade. Sprinkle the pork with the salt and pepper. Cook half of the pork in a single layer in the hot oil until lightly browned and cooked through, about 1 ½ minutes, turning occasionally. Repeat with the remaining coconut oil and pork.

3 Transfer the pork to a serving platter, and top with the scallions, cilantro, radishes, and remaining cucumber slices. Spoon about 2 tablespoons of the rice onto each lettuce leaf; top with the pork mixture and remaining rice.

COCONUT RICE

HANDS-ON: **5 MINUTES**   TOTAL: **55 MINUTES**   SERVES **4**

VG GF DF

1 cup uncooked brown basmati or jasmine rice

2 cups coconut milk

¼ teaspoon kosher salt

Rinse the rice with cold water; drain. Combine the rice, coconut milk, and salt in a saucepan. Bring to a boil over medium; cover and reduce the heat to low. Simmer until the liquid is absorbed, about 40 minutes. Remove from the heat, and let stand 10 minutes. Fluff with a fork.

MARINATED TRI-TIP STEAK WITH YAM FRIES AND DIJONNAISE

HANDS-ON: **30 MINUTES**   TOTAL: **1 HOUR**   SERVES **6**

Steak is de rigueur for game-day barbecues, and the tri-tip is a totally underrated version that is unbelievably flavorful—and won't break the bank. This recipe offers easy prep, fast cooking, a knockout sauce, and double-knockout mustard. The yam fries bring it home. Rich red wine probably not optional.

2 pounds yams or sweet potatoes, peeled and cut into ½-inch strips

1 tablespoon dry mustard

3 tablespoons raw honey

6 tablespoons grapeseed oil

3 tablespoons red wine vinegar

2 teaspoons chopped garlic cloves

1 teaspoon kosher salt

1 teaspoon black pepper

3 pounds beef tri-tip steak, cut into 6 portions

1 tablespoon ground cumin

2 teaspoons chipotle chile powder

Dijonnaise (recipe follows)

1 Preheat the oven to 400°F. Place the yam strips, dry mustard, honey, 3 tablespoons of the grapeseed oil, 2 tablespoons of the red wine vinegar, 1 teaspoon of the garlic, and ½ teaspoon each of the salt and pepper in a large bowl; toss to combine. Divide the mixture between 2 aluminum foil-lined rimmed baking sheets. Bake in preheated oven until golden brown, 30 to 40 minutes, rotating baking sheets top rack to bottom rack halfway through.

2 Meanwhile, whisk together 2 tablespoons of the oil and the remaining 1 tablespoon red wine vinegar. Pat the steak pieces dry; rub each with the oil mixture. Stir together the cumin, chile powder, remaining 1 teaspoon garlic, and remaining ½ teaspoon each salt and pepper in a small bowl. Sprinkle on both sides of the steaks.

3 Heat the remaining 1 tablespoon oil in a heavy, ovenproof 12-inch skillet over medium-high. Sear the steaks in the hot oil, about 1 minute and 30 seconds per side. Transfer the skillet to the upper third of the oven; bake until medium-rare, 6 to 8 minutes. Transfer the steaks to a platter; let rest about 4 minutes before serving. Serve with the yam fries and Dijonnaise.

DIJONNAISE

HANDS-ON: **5 MINUTES**   TOTAL: **5 MINUTES**   SERVES **6**

½ cup olive oil mayonnaise

3 tablespoons plain Greek-style yogurt

2 tablespoons Dijon mustard

Combine all the ingredients and serve.

CHILE-RUBBED SKIRT STEAK WITH RUSTIC CHIMICHURRI

HANDS-ON: **20 MINUTES**   TOTAL: **20 MINUTES**   SERVES **4**   GF   DF

Steak with chimichurri is a classic combo. The bright, fresh herb topping contrasts beautifully with the smoky, spicy steak.

2 tablespoons sherry vinegar

½ teaspoon lime zest, plus
   1 tablespoon fresh juice (from
   1 lime)

6 tablespoons olive oil

¼ cup torn fresh flat-leaf parsley

¼ cup torn fresh cilantro

2 tablespoons torn fresh mint

2 tablespoons minced shallots

1 teaspoon fine sea salt

¾ teaspoon black pepper

1 ½ teaspoons ancho chile powder

½ teaspoon red chile flakes

1 pound skirt steak

1 Preheat grill to medium-high (about 450°F). Whisk together the sherry vinegar, zest, juice, and ¼ cup of the oil in a small bowl. Stir in the parsley, cilantro, mint, shallots, and ¼ teaspoon each of the salt and pepper.

2 Combine the ancho chile powder, red chile flakes, and remaining ¾ teaspoon salt and ½ teaspoon pepper in a small bowl. Rub the steak with the remaining 2 tablespoons oil; sprinkle both sides of the steak with the spice mixture. Grill, uncovered, to desired degree of doneness, 2 to 3 minutes per side. Let stand 10 minutes; cut diagonally across the grain into thin slices. Serve with the chimichurri.

PROTEINS ON THE GROUND AND OUT OF THE SURF

MAPLE-and-TURMERIC-MARINATED PORK CHOPS with PICKLED CARROTS and DAIKON

HANDS-ON: 30 MINUTES   TOTAL: **30 MINUTES, PLUS 8 HOURS CHILLING**   SERVES **4**   **GF**

This filling dish mixes savory pork with bright, fresh pickles. The pickles can be made up to 3 days ahead.

- ¾ cup plain yogurt (not Greek-style)
- 2 teaspoons grated peeled turmeric root
- 1 tablespoon grated garlic
- ½ cup pure maple syrup
- 4 (½-pound) bone-in pork chops (about 1 ½ inches thick)
- 1 teaspoon black pepper
- 3 ½ teaspoons kosher salt
- 8 ounces carrots, peeled and cut into matchsticks
- 1 large daikon, trimmed and cut into matchsticks
- 1 cup apple cider vinegar
- 1 cup water
- 1 (1-inch) piece ginger, peeled and sliced
- 2 teaspoons yellow mustard seeds
- 2 tablespoons peanut oil

1 Combine the yogurt, turmeric, garlic, and ¼ cup of the maple syrup in a large zip-top plastic freezer bag. Sprinkle the pork with the pepper and 2 teaspoons of the salt. Place the pork chops in the bag with the marinade; seal and turn to coat. Chill, turning occasionally, at least 8 hours or overnight.

2 Place the carrots and daikon in a medium bowl. Combine the vinegar, 1 cup water, ginger, mustard seeds, and remaining ¼ cup maple syrup and 1 ½ teaspoons salt in a small saucepan. Bring to a simmer over medium-high. Pour the mixture over the carrots and daikon in the bowl. Cool to room temperature; cover and chill at least 8 hours or overnight.

3 Preheat the oven to 400°F. Remove the pork from the marinade; discard the marinade. Heat the oil in a large ovenproof skillet over medium-high. Add the pork chops; cook until deep golden brown, about 4 minutes. Turn the pork chops, and transfer the skillet to the preheated oven. Bake until a meat thermometer inserted into thickest portion registers 140°F, about 5 minutes. Remove from the oven; let stand 10 minutes. Serve with the pickled daikon and carrots.

ITALIAN SHRIMP AND GRITS WITH PANCETTA AND HEIRLOOM TOMATOES

HANDS-ON: **25 MINUTES**   TOTAL: **35 MINUTES**   SERVES **4**   **GF**

Shrimp and grits is a classic comfort dish for a reason: it's just so good and satisfying. Try swapping in millet grits for added nutrition.

2 cups unsalted chicken stock

1 cup unsweetened rice milk

1 cup uncooked stone-ground grits

½ cup cream cheese

1 ounce Parmesan cheese, shredded (about ¼ cup)

¼ teaspoon hot sauce

¾ teaspoon fine sea salt

½ teaspoon black pepper

2 ounces diced pancetta

1 ½ pounds peeled and deveined large raw shrimp

2 garlic cloves, minced

2 cups seeds removed and chopped heirloom tomatoes

1 tablespoon unsalted butter

2 tablespoons torn fresh flat-leaf parsley

1 tablespoon torn fresh oregano

1 Bring the chicken stock and rice milk to a boil in a saucepan over medium-high; whisk in the grits. Reduce the heat to medium; cover and cook until thickened and the grits are tender, 10 to 15 minutes. Remove from the heat; stir in the cream cheese, Parmesan, hot sauce, ½ teaspoon of the salt, and ¼ teaspoon of the pepper. Cover to keep warm.

2 Heat a large nonstick skillet over medium. Add the pancetta, and cook, stirring often, until browned and crisp, 6 to 8 minutes. Transfer to a plate lined with paper towels to drain, reserving drippings in the skillet. Increase the heat to medium-high. Add the shrimp and garlic to the skillet; cook until the shrimp are lightly browned and almost done, about 3 minutes. Add the tomatoes, and cook until the shrimp turn pink and the tomatoes begin to release their juices, 2 to 3 minutes. Remove from the heat; stir in the butter and remaining ¼ teaspoon each salt and pepper. Divide the grits among 4 bowls; top with the shrimp mixture. Sprinkle with the pancetta, parsley, and oregano.

SQUID-AND-CRAB SALAD

HANDS-ON: **30 MINUTES**   TOTAL: **30 MINUTES**   SERVES **6**   **GF** **DF**

*My mother once lived in New York's Little Italy, where she fell in love
with the fresh seafood, especially the squid. Well, I am my mother's
son: I love just about any kind of seafood, especially crab. With a little
inspiration from the West Coast classic, Crab Louie, I've put together
this vibrant mixture of our mother-and-son favorites, squid and crab,
complemented by a dressing that will knock your socks off.*

DRESSING

½ cup fresh pineapple juice

2 (1-inch) pieces fresh ginger,
  peeled and grated

1 to 2 serrano chiles, seeds
  removed, chopped

3 garlic cloves, smashed and
  chopped

2 tablespoons water

1 tablespoon finely chopped fresh
  lemongrass

1 tablespoon date sugar

1 tablespoon fish sauce

1 tablespoon hot chili oil or
  grapeseed oil

SALAD

2 quarts low-sodium or homemade
  chicken broth

1 pound fresh squid, cleaned,
  sliced into ⅓-inch rings, soaked
  in whole milk

½ pound fresh jumbo lump
  crabmeat

½ cup very thinly sliced red onion

1 cup shredded peeled daikon

2 carrots, peeled and shredded

½cup loosely packed fresh basil
  leaves, chopped

½ cup seeds removed and diced
  fresh cucumber

½ cup loosely packed fresh cilantro
  leaves, chopped

10 ounces fresh mixed greens

1 To prepare the Dressing: Process the pineapple juice, ginger,
serrano chiles, garlic, 2 tablespoons water, lemongrass, date sugar,
fish sauce, and hot chili oil in a blender until smooth. Set aside.

2 To prepare the Salad: Bring the broth to a boil over high. Add
the squid, and cook about 1 minute, while the water returns to a
simmer. Remove from the heat. Let the squid stand in the water
1 minute; drain and cool.

3 Pick the crabmeat, removing any bits of shell. Combine the squid,
crab, onion, daikon, carrots, basil, cucumber, and cilantro in a large
bowl. Add the dressing, and toss very gently once or twice. Serve
over the mixed greens.

IRON SKILLET SHRIMP WITH GRAPEFRUIT

HANDS-ON: **20 MINUTES**   TOTAL: **20 MINUTES**   SERVES **4**   **DF**

All I can say about this dish is that it just wins. Try it. You'll see what I mean.

1 pink grapefruit

¼ cup rice vinegar

1 tablespoon fresh lime juice (from 1 lime)

2 teaspoons Dijon mustard

2 teaspoons raw honey

1 teaspoon grated peeled fresh ginger

½ teaspoon kosher salt

½ teaspoon black pepper

½ cup plus 1 tablespoon olive oil

1 ½ pounds peeled and deveined large raw shrimp

1 teaspoon paprika

1 teaspoon ground cumin

5 ounces seasonal lettuce or greens (something with bite and body, such as arugula or spinach)

½ cup loosely packed fresh cilantro leaves

¼ cup thinly sliced red onion

¼ cup lightly toasted hazelnuts (loose skins rubbed off), chopped

1 Using a sharp knife, peel the grapefruit, and remove all pith. Carefully slice the fruit segments from the membrane.

2 Whisk together the vinegar, lime juice, mustard, honey, ginger, and ¼ teaspoon each of the salt and pepper in a large bowl. Add ½ cup of the oil in a slow, steady stream, whisking constantly to combine.

3 Sprinkle the shrimp with the paprika, cumin, and remaining ¼ teaspoon each salt and pepper. Heat the remaining 1 tablespoon oil in a large cast-iron or nonstick skillet over medium. Add the shrimp, and cook just until the shrimp turn pink, about 2 minutes per side.

4 Add the grapefruit, shrimp, greens, cilantro, onion, and hazelnuts to the vinaigrette in the bowl. Toss well.

CAST-IRON SKILLET WILD SALMON WITH NORI-MARINATED SQUASH AND VIETNAMESE SAUCE

HANDS-ON: **45 MINUTES**   TOTAL: **45 MINUTES, PLUS 8 HOURS CHILLING**   SERVES **4**   **GF** **DF**

Salmon is one of the essentials of clean eating—not to mention one of the great culinary pleasures—but it's important for reasons of sustainability to make sure you know what you're getting (check www.seafoodwatch.org). This dish takes inspiration from a cucumber teriyaki dish that is a staple of traditional Japanese cuisine, and it is clean, clean, clean—and as light as can be—while the dipping sauce adds a palette of spicy accents.

1 cup torn fresh Thai basil

1 cup torn fresh mint

2 tablespoons chopped peeled fresh ginger

¼ cup chili vinegar (or make your own, page 235)

¼ cup mirin

¼ cup tamari

5 nori sheets, crumbled into small pieces

3 garlic cloves, thinly sliced

7 tablespoons olive oil

1 large yellow zucchini, chopped

1 delicata squash, chopped

1 jalapeño chile, thinly sliced

4 (4-ounce) skin-on center-cut wild salmon fillets

1 teaspoon kosher salt

1 teaspoon black pepper

1 shallot, thinly sliced

2 garlic cloves, thinly sliced

Vietnamese Sauce (recipe follows, page 160)

1 Stir together the basil, mint, ginger, chili vinegar, mirin, tamari, nori, garlic, and 3 tablespoons of the olive oil in a large bowl. Add the zucchini and delicata squash; cover and chill at least 8 hours or overnight. (The marinade will get absorbed.)

2 Preheat the oven to 400°F. Combine the jalapeño slices and 1 tablespoon of the oil in a small bowl. Set aside.

3 Sprinkle the salmon with ½ teaspoon each of the salt and pepper. Heat 2 tablespoons of the oil in a large cast-iron or ovenproof skillet over medium-high. Add the salmon fillets, skin side down, and cook 3 minutes. Transfer the skillet to the oven, and bake until the salmon is cooked through, about 5 minutes.

4 Heat a large skillet over medium-high. Add the squash and zucchini; cook, without stirring, until the vegetables begin to caramelize, about 3 minutes. Remove from the heat; sprinkle with the remaining ½ teaspoon each salt and pepper. Transfer to a bowl.

5 Wipe the skillet clean, and add the remaining 1 tablespoon oil. Heat over medium-high. Add the shallot and garlic; cook until crisp and golden, about 2 minutes. Transfer to a plate lined with paper towels to drain.

6 Divide the squash and zucchini among 4 plates. Top each with 1 salmon fillet. Sprinkle with the toasted shallot and garlic. Top each salmon fillet with the oil-soaked jalapeño slices. Drizzle with the Vietnamese Sauce.

Continued

VIETNAMESE SAUCE

HANDS-ON: **10 MINUTES**   TOTAL: **10 MINUTES**   MAKES ½ **CUP**   **DF**

¼ cup chili vinegar (or make your
  own, page 235)

2 tablespoons rice vinegar

2 tablespoons fresh lime juice

2 tablespoons sesame oil

2 tablespoons sambal oelek
  (ground fresh chile paste)

1 tablespoon coconut sugar

1 tablespoon raw honey

1 teaspoon fish sauce

¼ cup grapeseed oil or olive oil

2 tablespoons finely chopped
  fresh lemongrass

Process the chili vinegar, rice vinegar, lime juice, sesame oil, sambal
oelek, sugar, honey, and fish sauce in a blender until smooth, about
5 seconds. With the blender running, slowly pour in the grapeseed
oil and process until smooth. Transfer to a small bowl; stir in the
lemongrass.

SUSTAINABLY
RAISED MEAT AND SEAFOOD?
HOW CAN YOU BE SURE?

THERE'S A GREAT WAY to learn all about sustainable seafood and to keep track of the suppliers and restaurants that serve it, and that's the Monterey Bay Aquarium's Seafood Watch mobile app, available for both iOS and Android at the App Store or Google Play. I recommend it wholeheartedly. It lets you find out about any kind of seafood or sushi from A to Z—and check its sustainability status—and it will help you find places near you, wherever you are, where you can buy or dine on sustainable seafood.

With beef, you'll have to work a little harder, but the first step is to develop a relationship with your local butcher, express your concern, ask the provenance of the meat on offer, and let the butcher know that you and your family want only beef that was humanely raised and grass-fed.

Ditto for chicken: Let your local market know you're only buying free-range, hormone-free chickens fed no antibiotics at all! The reason? You and your kids know that if we eat animals that have been force-fed antibiotics, those life-saving medicines may not work for us when we need them.

Want to know even more? Check out Supermoms Against Superbugs (www.saveantibiotics.org) and meet my friend and colleague, award-winning chef Suzanne Goin, who is leading the campaign to rein in the use of antibiotics in industrial farming.

HALIBUT over APPLES and PECANS with HONEY MUSTARD VINAIGRETTE

HANDS-ON: **45 MINUTES**   TOTAL: **45 MINUTES**   SERVES **4**   **GF** **DF**

I was strolling through the farmers' market one fall day in 2015—a bumper year for apples—and I just couldn't resist the apples' tart freshness. So I bought up a bunch and challenged myself to come up with something delicious. The idea for the halibut came to me on the walk home, and the details kind of wrote themselves. I hope you'll agree that I rose to the challenge with pretty awesome results.

3 tablespoons bacon drippings

2 ripe Granny Smith apples, peeled and cut into 1 ½-inch pieces

2 large turnips, peeled and cut into 1 ½-inch pieces

1 ¾ teaspoons kosher salt

¾ teaspoon black pepper

⅓ cup sliced red onion

2 garlic cloves, finely chopped

1 bunch Swiss chard, stems and leaves finely chopped

3 tablespoons hazelnut oil or olive oil

2 tablespoons red wine vinegar

1 tablespoon whole-grain mustard

1 tablespoon raw honey

½ cup toasted chopped pecans

4 (5-ounce) skinless halibut fillets

1 Preheat the oven to 400°F. Heat 2 tablespoons of the bacon drippings in a large nonstick skillet. Add the apples and turnips; cook, stirring often, until golden-brown and soft, 6 to 8 minutes. Stir in ½ teaspoon of the salt and ¼ teaspoon of the pepper. Transfer to a plate lined with paper towels. Add the onion and garlic to the skillet; cook until the onion is translucent, 2 to 3 minutes. Add the chard; cook, stirring often, until the chard is wilted, about 1 minute. Remove from the heat.

2 Whisk together the oil, vinegar, mustard, honey, and ¼ teaspoon each salt and pepper in a bowl. Stir in ¼ cup of the pecans.

3 Heat the remaining 1 tablespoon bacon drippings in an ovenproof nonstick skillet over medium-high. Pat the fish dry with paper towels. Sprinkle both sides of the fillets with the remaining 1 teaspoon salt and ¼ teaspoon pepper. Add the fillets to the skillet in a single layer, and cook until the edges begin to brown, 5 to 6 minutes. Transfer the skillet to the preheated oven, and bake until the fish is no longer translucent, about 2 minutes.

4 Divide the apples and turnips among 4 plates; place a handful of the chard mixture beside the apples and turnips. Top each with 1 halibut fillet. Spoon about 1 tablespoon of the honey-mustard mixture over each fillet, and sprinkle each with 1 tablespoon pecans.

SMOKED TROUT WITH CELERY ROOT, PEAR, AND JERUSALEM ARTICHOKES

HANDS-ON: **20 MINUTES**　TOTAL: **40 MINUTES**　SERVES **6**

What was once a way to preserve fish—curing it with smoke—is now an art performed for the unique taste it achieves. In New York, varieties of smoked salmon and whitefish are so popular they're almost everyday items, but smoked trout is a less well-known treat. This recipe shows off its awesome flavor, while the Jerusalem artichokes have enough taste and body to stand up to the fish.

3 medium Jerusalem artichokes, peeled, quartered, and thinly sliced

1 medium celery root, peeled and cut into ½-inch pieces

1 Bosc pear, peeled and cut into ½-inch pieces

2 tablespoons olive oil

1 ½ teaspoons kosher salt

½ teaspoon black pepper

⅓ cup plain Greek-style yogurt

¼ cup grated fresh horseradish

4 tablespoons chopped fresh basil

2 tablespoons chili vinegar (or make your own, page 235)

1 tablespoon coconut sugar

⅛ teaspoon chili powder

6 ounces boneless, skinless smoked trout, flaked into 1-inch pieces

12 ounces microgreens (such as amaranth, kale, or celery)

3 cups baby lettuce

Lemon slices

1 Preheat the oven to 400°F. Toss together the Jerusalem artichokes, celery root, pear, oil, 1 teaspoon of the salt, and ¼ teaspoon of the pepper on a rimmed baking sheet. Roast in preheated oven until tender, about 20 minutes.

2 Whisk together the yogurt, horseradish, basil, vinegar, coconut sugar, chili powder, and remaining ½ teaspoon salt and ¼ teaspoon pepper in a bowl. Toss the trout with 2 tablespoons of the yogurt mixture in a separate bowl.

3 Place the roasted vegetables on a serving platter. Top with the trout mixture, microgreens, and lettuce. Serve with the lemon slices and remaining yogurt mixture.

6
THE VEGETABLE FIX

All veg all the time. Here are recipes for vegetable mains and accompaniments. Use these recipes to put vegetables on skewers or in bowls, to offer a vegetable buffet, or to create a plant-forward tasting menu if you like. You might also mix and match any of these recipes with protein choices from Chapter 5 or stick to vegetables from start to finish: it is your choice.

As much as you can, source your vegetables—fresh—from farmers' markets or other local suppliers. Look for a range of vibrant, colorful, firm products, the true bounty of the earth. Essential to our health and well-being, vegetables are also essential to fine home cooking, and the recipes of this chapter will give your culinary creativity a workout you and your family will appreciate.

CANDIED TURNIPS AND SWEET POTATOES WITH YUZU

HANDS-ON: **10 MINUTES**   TOTAL: **1 HOUR, 25 MINUTES**   SERVES **4**   VG GF DF

As a Southern boy, I grew up on candied vegetables, so popular in that part of the country. But where the traditional Southern way to candy a veg is with brown sugar, I use yuzu and maple syrup, which do the job just as sweetly but more healthfully. Turnips are another Southern throwback, and as far as I'm concerned, you can never get enough.

1 pound sweet potatoes or garnet yams, peeled

1 pound turnips, peeled

3 strips orange peel

2 (3-inch) cinnamon sticks, broken in half

¼ cup bottled yuzu juice

3 tablespoons pure maple syrup

1 tablespoon pure olive oil

½ tablespoon sesame oil

½ tablespoon fresh lemon juice (from 1 lemon)

1 teaspoon finely chopped fresh ginger

½ teaspoon coarse sea salt

⅓ teaspoon black pepper

1 cup loosely packed fresh basil leaves, torn

1 Preheat the oven to 375°F.

2 Cut the sweet potatoes and turnips in half crosswise; cut each half lengthwise into 2 (½-inch) wedges. Toss together the sweet potatoes, turnips, orange peel strips, and cinnamon stick pieces on a rimmed baking sheet.

3 Whisk together the yuzu juice, maple syrup, oils, lemon juice, and ginger. Drizzle ¼ cup of the marinade over the sweet potato mixture; sprinkle with the salt and pepper, and toss to coat. Spread the mixture in an even layer on the baking sheet.

4 Bake in preheated oven until the sweet potatoes and turnips are tender and glazed, about 1 hour and 15 minutes, brushing the vegetables with the remaining marinade every 15 minutes. Remove the orange peel strips and cinnamon stick pieces, and sprinkle with the torn basil before serving.

CRISPY GREEN TOMATOES

HANDS-ON: **10 MINUTES**   TOTAL: **10 MINUTES**   SERVES **6**   (V) (GF)

The traditional Southern recipe uses white flour, but this summer side is just as good with brown rice flour, which makes it gluten-free.

1 large egg

½ cup buttermilk

¾ cup (about 4 ounces) stone-ground cornmeal

½ teaspoon black pepper

¾ cup (about 3.75 ounces) brown rice flour

1 ¼ teaspoons fine sea salt

3 large green tomatoes, cut into ¼-inch-thick slices

Peanut oil

Lemon wedges

1 Stir together the egg and buttermilk in a shallow dish. Combine the cornmeal, pepper, ½ cup of the brown rice flour, and 1 teaspoon of the salt in a second dish. Place the remaining ¼ cup brown rice flour in a third dish.

2 Dredge the tomato slices in the brown rice flour; dip in the buttermilk mixture, and dredge in the cornmeal mixture.

3 Pour the oil to a depth of ¼ inch in a Dutch oven or cast-iron skillet; heat to 375°F. Fry the tomato slices in the hot oil, in batches, until golden brown, about 2 minutes per side. Drain on paper towels. Sprinkle the tomatoes with the remaining ¼ teaspoon salt, and serve with the lemon wedges.

100% REAL

ROASTED HEIRLOOM CARROTS WITH WATERCRESS AND MISO VINAIGRETTE

HANDS-ON: **15 MINUTES**   TOTAL: **35 MINUTES**   SERVES **4** (V) (GF) (DF)

Heirloom carrots come in different shapes and colors. They also taste sweeter than the ones you're used to seeing in the supermarket, especially when roasted.

1 pound assorted heirloom carrots, trimmed and peeled
¼ cup extra-virgin olive oil
¾ teaspoon kosher salt
¾ teaspoon black pepper
2 tablespoons rice vinegar
1 tablespoon white miso
1 tablespoon raw honey
1 cup packed watercress

1 Preheat the oven to 450°F. Bring a large pot of water fitted with a steamer basket to a boil over high. Place the carrots in the basket, and steam until mostly tender, about 5 minutes. Transfer the carrots to a bowl. Add 2 tablespoons of the olive oil and ½ teaspoon each of the salt and pepper; toss to coat. Arrange the carrot mixture on a baking sheet. Roast in the preheated oven until browned, about 20 minutes, turning the carrots after 15 minutes.

2 Meanwhile, whisk together the vinegar, miso, honey, remaining 2 tablespoons oil, and remaining ¼ teaspoon each salt and pepper.

3 Place the carrots on a serving platter. Top with the watercress, and drizzle with the vinaigrette.

SWEET-and-SOUR RED LENTILS with PEAS, HERBS, and COCONUT

HANDS-ON: **20 MINUTES** TOTAL: **30 MINUTES** SERVES **4** Ⓥ ⒼⒻ

Humans in every part of the world have been eating lentils for 15,000 years, but I'm betting that this recipe is a first. Looks like a salad, but you just won't believe the blend of clashing tastes—not to mention nutritional value that's off the charts. Throw some other crunchy things on top, too—like fried shallots or leeks—for an extra touch.

2 cups uncooked red lentils, rinsed

3 tablespoons unsalted butter

½ cup thinly sliced celery, cut on the diagonal

3 shallots, diced

2 garlic cloves, thinly sliced on a mandoline (about 1 tablespoon)

1 cup coconut milk

¼ cup rice vinegar

2 tablespoons olive oil

2 tablespoons sambal oelek

2 tablespoons bottled yuzu juice

1 cup green peas (fresh or frozen, thawed)

½ cup thinly sliced fresh basil strips

⅓ cup thinly sliced fresh mint strips

1 cup loosely packed fresh arugula

½ teaspoon fine sea salt

½ teaspoon black pepper

1 Bring 4 quarts water to a boil in an 8-quart stockpot; add the lentils, and boil until tender, 18 to 20 minutes. Drain the lentils well, and transfer to a bowl.

2 Melt the butter in a large nonstick skillet over medium-high. Add the celery, shallots, and garlic, and cook, stirring often, until softened, 5 to 7 minutes. Add the lentils, coconut milk, rice vinegar, oil, sambal oelek, yuzu juice, peas, basil, and mint to the skillet, and cook until heated through, about 5 minutes. Add the arugula, stirring just until wilted. Stir in the salt and pepper.

CHINESE LONG BEANS WITH SESAME AND RUTABAGA CAPONATA

HANDS-ON: **30 MINUTES**   TOTAL: **40 MINUTES**   SERVES **4**   VG GF DF

Long beans are one of my all-time favorite ingredients. I love their texture, their density, their color, and the fact that they do so well no matter how you cook them—braised, grilled, roasted, sautéed: you name it, long beans are great. But you won't see long beans paired with caponata, a classic Italian dish, anywhere except in this book, nor would you see the words "sesame oil" and "caponata" in the same sentence anywhere else. Yet I promise you're going to find this mesh of cuisines absolutely delicious.

½ pound rutabaga, peeled and sliced into ⅓-inch-thick rounds

½ pound eggplant, sliced into ⅓-inch-thick rounds

6 fresh tomatoes (about 1 pound), cut into ⅓-inch-thick rounds

1 pound Chinese long beans (also called snake beans), cut in half

⅓ cup sesame oil

½ cup thinly sliced red onion

3 garlic cloves

2 tablespoons capers, drained

3 tablespoons red wine vinegar

1 cup canned San Marzano tomatoes, undrained

2 tablespoons black sesame seeds

1 teaspoon fine sea salt

1 cup arugula

1 to 2 teaspoons red chile flakes

1 Preheat a gas grill to medium (about 400°F) or heat a grill pan to medium-high.

2 Place the rutabagas on an oiled grill grate, and grill, uncovered, until tender, 5 to 7 minutes per side. At the same time, grill the eggplant until tender, 4 to 5 minutes per side, and grill the tomatoes until tender, 1 to 2 ½ minutes per side. Add the long beans, and grill until tender-crisp, 1 ½ to 2 ½ minutes per side, using a grill basket, if necessary. Transfer the grilled vegetables to a cutting board, and let cool.

3 Heat the sesame oil in a large skillet over medium-high until hot. Add the onion, and cook, stirring often, until translucent, about 1 minute. Add the garlic and capers, and cook, stirring often, until translucent and golden, 2 to 3 minutes.

4 Chop the cooled rutabaga, eggplant, and tomato rounds, and add with the vinegar, canned tomatoes, black sesame seeds, and salt to the skillet. Reduce the heat to low, and simmer the mixture, stirring occasionally, until the liquid is reduced by about one-third, about 20 minutes.

5 Add the long beans to the skillet, and cook, stirring often, 2 minutes. Serve the hot bean mixture with the arugula; sprinkle with the red chile flakes. Or chill the mixture, and serve cold.

PEA SHOOT SALAD WITH CELERY, SESAME, AND CHINESE BLACK VINEGAR

HANDS-ON: **5 MINUTES**   TOTAL: **5 MINUTES**   SERVES **4**   VG GF DF

You can find fresh, lightly sweet pea shoots at farm stands or Asian markets. They are a nice addition to salads, stir-fries, and soups.

1 tablespoon sesame oil

1 teaspoon grated fresh ginger

1 garlic clove, grated

½ cup thinly sliced celery

1 pound fresh pea shoots, trimmed into 2-inch-long pieces

1 tablespoon Chinese black vinegar

1 ½ tablespoons toasted sesame seeds

½ teaspoon fine sea salt

⅛ teaspoon black pepper

Heat the sesame oil in a large skillet over medium-high. Add the ginger, and cook, stirring often, until softened, about 2 minutes. Add the garlic and celery; cook, stirring often, 1 minute. Remove from the heat. Toss with the pea shoots. Drizzle with the vinegar, and sprinkle with the sesame seeds, salt, and pepper.

TERIYAKI CUCUMBERS with LIME, JALAPEÑO, and CILANTRO

HANDS-ON: **15 MINUTES**   TOTAL: **15 MINUTES**   SERVES **4**   (V) (GF) (DF)

Cucumbers are hydrating, rich in potassium, and have anti-inflammatory properties. The homemade teriyaki sauce here elevates the freshness of this simple and quick salad to the next level.

½ cup tamari

3 tablespoons raw honey

2 tablespoons water

2 tablespoons sweet rice wine

2 tablespoons coconut sugar

1 garlic clove, chopped

1 teaspoon minced fresh ginger

2 cups sliced English cucumber (about 9.5 ounces)

½ cup thinly sliced red onion

½ cup loosely packed fresh cilantro leaves

1 medium-size jalapeño chile, seeds removed, minced

1 lime

2 teaspoons sesame oil

1 teaspoon rice vinegar

1 teaspoon black sesame seeds

1 Stir together the tamari, honey, 2 tablespoons water, rice wine, coconut sugar, garlic, and ginger in a small saucepan over medium-high; bring to a simmer. Reduce the heat to low, and cook until the mixture is reduced by half, about 10 minutes. Transfer the mixture to a bowl to cool. (The homemade teriyaki will thicken as it cools.)

2 Combine the cucumber, onion, cilantro leaves, and jalapeño in a large bowl.

3 Grate the zest from the lime into a small bowl; squeeze the juice from the lime into the bowl. Add the sesame oil, rice vinegar, and 2 tablespoons of the homemade teriyaki, and whisk together. Pour the teriyaki dressing mixture over the cucumber mixture, and toss to coat. Sprinkle with the sesame seeds, and serve. Store the remaining homemade teriyaki in an airtight container for 1 week in the refrigerator.

ZUCCHINI "PASTA" WITH GREEN GODDESS VINAIGRETTE

HANDS-ON: **25 MINUTES**   TOTAL: **30 MINUTES**   SERVES **6**   **GF**

You may already know I'm a big advocate for alternatives to the traditional durum flour-based pasta, whether it's shiitake noodle flour or rice flour or this beautiful choice. Through the miracle of the spiralizer, zucchini comes out shaped like spaghetti, creating a "pasta" that's hearty enough to be the main course and light enough to be a side dish or snack. Serve it piping hot, at room temperature, or cold—and if you let it sit overnight, it'll be even better.

Green Goddess is a vinaigrette as sophisticated as it is clean. At its heart are avocados—delicious and there is nothing better for your skin, your heart, or your health—and around them is a unique combination of ingredients that lets each flavor stand out against the other.

8 zucchini

1 teaspoon fine sea salt

2 ripe avocados, coarsely chopped

¼ cup chili vinegar (or make your own, page 235)

1 ½ tablespoons raw honey

1 tablespoon fresh lime juice

5 tablespoons coconut oil, melted

2 garlic cloves, smashed and chopped

3 cups loosely packed fresh basil leaves, chopped

2 cups loosely packed fresh mint leaves, chopped

4 cups pear tomatoes, sliced

½ cup pine nuts, chopped

1 ounce shaved Parmesan cheese (about ½ cup)

1 Using a spiralizer, turn the zucchini into noodles. Or, using a julienne peeler, peel the zucchini lengthwise into long strips, stopping at the inside part containing the seeds; discard the seeds. Sprinkle the zucchini noodles with ½ teaspoon of the salt, and let stand until softened.

2 Process the avocados, chili vinegar, honey, lime juice, and 2 tablespoons of the melted coconut oil with a handheld blender or regular blender until smooth. Stir the remaining ½ teaspoon salt into the vinaigrette.

3 Gently stir together the zucchini noodles and remaining 3 tablespoons of the melted coconut oil in a large skillet over medium-high. Add the garlic, and cook, stirring occasionally, 2 minutes.

4 Toss together 1 ½ cups of the vinaigrette, 2 ½ cups of the chopped basil, and 1 ½ cups of the chopped mint in a large serving bowl. Add the zucchini mixture to the serving bowl. Top with the tomatoes, pine nuts, Parmesan cheese, and remaining ½ cup each basil and mint.

Use the remaining vinaigrette as a dip with fresh vegetables or pita chips.

ZUCCHINI NOODLES WITH FAVA BEANS, MINT, AND GARLIC

HANDS-ON: **30 MINUTES**   TOTAL: **35 MINUTES**   SERVES **4**   Ⓥ ⒼⒻ

This is an easy and light vegetarian meal that comes together quickly. The mint with the salty ricotta salata is a combo that really pops.

1 ½ cups shelled fava beans (about 1 ½ pounds unshelled)

4 medium zucchini

2 tablespoons olive oil

3 garlic cloves, sliced

¼ teaspoon red chile flakes

¼ cup loosely packed fresh mint leaves

½ teaspoon fine sea salt

1 tablespoon fresh lemon juice, plus zest for garnish (from 1 lemon)

4 ounces crumbled ricotta salata cheese (about 1 cup)

Sliced scallion, optional

Chopped peanuts, optional

1 Bring a large saucepan of water to a boil. Add the fava beans, and cook 2 minutes; drain. Place the beans in a large bowl of ice water to cool; drain well. Remove the tough outer green skins from the beans; discard the skins. Set the beans aside.

2 Using a spiralizer, turn zucchini into noodles. Or, using a julienne peeler, peel the zucchini lengthwise into strips to equal about 7 cups, discarding the seeds.

3 Heat the oil in a large nonstick skillet over medium-high. Add the garlic and red chile flakes; cook, stirring often, 1 minute. Add the zucchini; cook, stirring often, 2 minutes. Remove from the heat; stir in the mint, salt, fava beans, and lemon juice. Sprinkle with the ricotta salata, lemon zest, and, if desired, scallion and peanuts.

TIP

Substitute edamame for the fava beans.

BOK CHOY with OYSTER MUSHROOMS

HANDS-ON: **35 MINUTES**   TOTAL: **35 MINUTES**   SERVES **4**   VG GF DF

One of the routines I've developed as a New Yorker is wandering up and down the streets of Chinatown to check out what's available in the market stalls there, since it is so different from what's to be found in the humongous Union Square Greenmarket in Manhattan or the McCarren Park market in my Brooklyn neighborhood. What always knocks me for a loop is the amount and variety of the greens, especially the bok choy. This dish derives from that experience—and from the influence of Chinese cuisine on cooking in New York.

4 teaspoons fine salt

1 large bunch (about 2 pounds) bok choy

1 tablespoon olive oil

¼ cup ¼-inch-thick diagonally cut celery slices

2 large garlic cloves, thinly sliced

2 tablespoons finely chopped shallot

1 tablespoon chopped fresh ginger

4 to 6 ounces oyster mushrooms, thinly sliced

1 teaspoon finely chopped jalapeño chile, optional

2 teaspoons tamari

¼ cup chopped fresh cilantro

1 tablespoon chili vinegar (or make your own, page 235)

¼ cup roasted pumpkin seeds (pepitas)

1 lemon, cut into wedges

1 Bring 4 quarts water to a boil in a stockpot or large Dutch oven over high. Add 2 teaspoons of the salt. Add the bok choy, and cook, uncovered, until bright green, about 15 seconds. Drain well, and set aside.

2 Heat the oil in a heavy-bottomed skillet over medium. Add the celery, garlic, shallot, and ginger, and cook, stirring often, until translucent, about 2 minutes. Add the mushrooms, jalapeño, if desired, and tamari, and cook, stirring occasionally, until the mushrooms soften, 2 to 3 minutes.

3 Chop the cooked bok choy, and add to the skillet; cook, stirring often, until tender, 1 to 2 minutes. Stir in the cilantro, vinegar, and remaining 2 teaspoons salt. Sprinkle with the pumpkin seeds, and serve with the lemon wedges on the side.

GRILLED MARINATED MELON with BOK CHOY, ROASTED SHALLOTS, and COCONUT MILK VINAIGRETTE

HANDS-ON: **20 MINUTES** TOTAL: **30 MINUTES** SERVES **4** GF DF V

Think summer grilling is all about burgers and barbecue? Think again.
Give vegetarians something to look forward to at your next cookout.

1 ½ tablespoons dark sesame oil

2 tablespoons raw honey

2 tablespoons fresh lime juice (from 1 lime)

½ teaspoon red chile flakes

3 tablespoons tamari

1 medium-size honeydew melon (rind removed), halved, and cut into 1-inch-thick slices

4 medium shallots, quartered through the root

4 baby bok choy, halved lengthwise

5 tablespoons peanut oil

½ cup full-fat coconut milk

1 ½ tablespoons rice vinegar

½ teaspoon fine sea salt

1 Preheat a gas grill to medium-high (about 450°F) on one side. Whisk together the sesame oil, honey, lime juice, red chile flakes, and 2 tablespoons of the tamari in a small bowl. Place the melon in a large baking dish, and pour 3 tablespoons to ¼ cup of the marinade over the melon slices, turning to coat.

2 Place the melon slices on an oiled grate over the lit side of the grill. Grill, uncovered, until grill marks appear, about 5 minutes. Turn and grill until grill marks appear, about 5 minutes. Remove the melon slices from the grill, and let stand until room temperature.

3 Toss the shallots with 1 tablespoon of the marinade, and place in the center of a piece of heavy-duty aluminum foil; wrap the foil around the shallots to form a packet. Place the packet on the grate over the unlit side of the grill. Cover and grill until the shallots are tender and slightly caramelized, 12 to 15 minutes.

4 Toss the bok choy halves with 1 tablespoon of the peanut oil, and place on the lit side of the grill. Grill, uncovered, until tender, about 5 to 8 minutes.

5 Meanwhile, whisk together the coconut milk, rice vinegar, salt, and remaining ¼ cup peanut oil and 1 tablespoon tamari in a bowl. Drizzle over the grilled melon, bok choy, and roasted shallots.

VERY COLD TOMATO SOUP
WITH BASIL

HANDS-ON: **15 MINUTES**   TOTAL: **2 HOURS, 15 MINUTES**   SERVES **6** **GF**

It's a hot, humid day on the East End of Long Island, but the farmers'
market is offering heirloom tomatoes, fresh basil, shallots, and garlic.
Here's how you cool off while warming up your taste buds.

4 pounds ripe, juicy, succulent
  heirloom or large vine-ripened
  tomatoes

2 tablespoons finely chopped
  shallot

1 teaspoon finely chopped garlic

5 tablespoons organic olive oil

1 tablespoon lemon zest, plus 2
  tablespoons fresh juice (from 1
  lemon)

1 teaspoon red wine vinegar

1 tablespoon raw honey

1 teaspoon ground coriander

1 teaspoon ground turmeric

1 ½ teaspoons black pepper

1 teaspoon sea salt

1 ½ cups loosely packed fresh
  basil, cut into thin strips

Freshly grated or shaved Parmesan
  cheese, optional

1 Roughly chop the tomatoes, reserving the juice. Process the
chopped tomatoes, shallot, and garlic in a food processor or blender
until smooth. (For a thinner, more refined soup, pour through a
fine wire-mesh strainer.) Transfer to a bowl, and stir in the olive
oil, lemon zest, lemon juice, vinegar, honey, coriander, turmeric,
pepper, and salt.

2 Cover and chill until very cold, at least 2 hours. Serve very cold in
soup bowls with the basil and, if desired, Parmesan.

EGGPLANT-and-ZUCCHINI PARMIGIANA

HANDS-ON: **30 MINUTES**   TOTAL: **1 HOUR**   SERVES **6** **GF**

You don't have to be Italian to love this dish, but I have one Italian-American buddy who eats it constantly. I thought it might be a good idea to find a cleaner way for him to enjoy the dish he has loved all his life, so he can keep on eating it for the rest of his life. This recipe provides the classic taste of the dish, but with ingredients like chickpea flour and almond milk, it does so with a lighter and healthier touch.

1 ½ pounds eggplant, cut into ⅓-inch-thick slices

½ pound yellow zucchini, cut into ½-inch-thick slices

2 teaspoons fine sea salt

½ cup unsweetened almond milk

5 large eggs

1 cup (about 3.25 ounces) chickpea flour

½ cup (about 2.5 ounces) brown rice flour

¼ cup (about 1.06 ounces) tapioca starch

1 teaspoon black pepper

1 cup olive oil

2 (15-ounce) cartons ricotta cheese (about 4 cups)

2 ½ ounces Parmesan cheese, finely grated (about 1 cup)

2 ounces ricotta salata, grated (about ½ cup)

2 ounces almond cheese, grated (about ½ cup)

¼ cup loosely packed fresh flat-leaf parsley leaves, chopped

2 tablespoons fresh thyme leaves, chopped

2 tablespoons fresh oregano leaves, chopped

4 cups tomato sauce

4 ounces low-fat mozzarella, grated (about 1 cup)

1 Arrange the eggplant and zucchini slices in a single layer on a baking sheet; sprinkle with 1 teaspoon of the salt. Cover with paper towels, and let stand 30 minutes.

2 Meanwhile, preheat the oven to 325°F. Stir together the almond milk and 4 of the eggs in a shallow dish.

3 Whisk together the flours, tapioca starch, and ½ teaspoon each of the salt and pepper in another shallow dish. Lightly dip the eggplant and zucchini slices on both sides in the egg mixture, letting the excess drip off. Dredge the slices in the flour mixture.

4 Heat ¼ cup of the oil in a 12-inch skillet over medium-high. Fry the vegetable slices, in batches, until golden brown, about 2 minutes per side, adding more oil, as needed.

5 Stir together the ricotta, Parmesan, ricotta salata, almond cheese, chopped herbs, and the remaining ½ teaspoon each salt and pepper.

6 Spread half of the tomato sauce over the bottom of a lightly greased 13- x 9-inch baking dish. Top with half each of the eggplant and zucchini slices, with the slices overlapping slightly. Spread half of the ricotta cheese-and-herb mixture over the vegetables. Repeat the layers once, ending with the ricotta cheese-and-herb mixture. Sprinkle the mozzarella over the top. Cover the baking dish with aluminum foil.

7 Bake in preheated oven 30 minutes. Uncover and bake until the mozzarella is lightly browned, about 10 minutes.

FALL VEGETABLES WITH ALMOND CREAM AND CRISPY GREENS

HANDS-ON: **30 MINUTES**   TOTAL: **30 MINUTES**   SERVES **6 TO 8**   (VG) (GF) (DF)

Here's another dish inspired by my walks through New York's farmers' markets and feeling challenged to make use of what I see. This is one of those warming dishes we look forward to when autumn rolls around, and it is a great accompaniment to different proteins—maybe a turkey pot pie, or Chapter 5's Halibut over Apples and Pecans with Honey Mustard Vinaigrette—page 163.

½ cup olive oil

½ cup thinly sliced red onion

2 tablespoons chopped garlic

1 cup chopped celery

1 cup chopped carrots

⅓ cup chopped peeled sweet potatoes

1 cup chopped peeled zucchini (seeds removed)

⅓ pound fresh cranberry beans in shells, shells removed, cooked

1 ½ cups unsweetened almond milk

1 tablespoon finely chopped jalapeño chile

1 tablespoon Champagne vinegar

1 tablespoon hazelnut oil

1 tablespoon lemon zest

¾ tablespoon fine sea salt

1 cup firmly packed fresh flat-leaf parsley leaves, chopped

1 cup firmly packed fresh basil leaves, torn in half

2 cups thinly sliced fresh bok choy

1 Heat the olive oil in a large skillet over medium-high. Add the onion and garlic, and cook, stirring often, until they start to become translucent, about 1 minute. Add the celery, carrots, and sweet potatoes, and cook, stirring often, until the mixture becomes very fragrant, about 5 minutes. Add the zucchini and cooked beans to the skillet, and cook, stirring often, just until the zucchini starts to become tender, about 2 minutes. Add the almond milk, and cook, stirring until the liquid is reduced to about ¼ cup, about 10 minutes. Set aside.

2 Whisk together the jalapeño, Champagne vinegar, hazelnut oil, lemon zest, and sea salt.

3 Place the herbs and cooked vegetable mixture in a large serving bowl. Fold in the dressing. Divide the vegetable mixture among the serving plates. Top with the sliced bok choy.

GRILLED SQUASH with PINE NUTS and BASIL

HANDS-ON: **10 MINUTES**   TOTAL: **40 MINUTES**   SERVES **6** 🄖🄕

Delicata squash is one of my go-to vegetables: you can leave the skin on, it holds up beautifully under any type of cooking—braising, roasting, grilling—and it's a great crowd-pleaser. If you can't find delicata squash, use butternut squash.

½ cup extra-virgin olive oil

½ cup coconut sugar

2 teaspoons kosher salt

2 teaspoons black pepper

4 medium delicata squash, seeds removed, cut into half-moons

¼ cup pine nuts, lightly toasted

½ cup loosely packed fresh basil leaves, torn into thin strips

1 ounce shaved Parmigiano-Reggiano cheese (about ¼ cup)

1 tablespoon orange zest

⅛ teaspoon red chile flakes, optional

2 lemons, cut into wedges

1 Preheat the grill to medium-high (about 450°F). Whisk together the olive oil, coconut sugar, and 1 teaspoon each of the salt and pepper until smooth.

2 Brush both sides of the delicata squash with the coconut sugar mixture. Place the squash on an oiled grate, and grill, uncovered and turning often, until golden brown, 8 to 12 minutes. (Rotate the squash pieces, as needed, from hot to cool spots so the pieces cook evenly and don't burn.)

3 Transfer the squash to a serving platter; sprinkle the top with the pine nuts, basil, cheese, orange zest, and, if desired, red chile flakes. Serve with the lemon wedges.

LASAGNA with TOMATO SAUCE, LOVELY ROASTED MUSHROOMS, and MELTED LEEKS

HANDS-ON: **35 MINUTES**   TOTAL: **1 HOUR, 30 MINUTES**   SERVES **6**

I'm partial to leeks because when well cooked, as in this recipe, they dissolve into the dish till they're an almost unseen essence. Yet they bring to this lasagna just the right undertone of onion sensation to complement the layered combination of mushrooms, cheese, and a totally banging tomato sauce.

9 uncooked lasagna noodles (about 8 ounces)

1 pound leeks

3 tablespoons extra-virgin olive oil, divided

3 carrots, peeled and finely diced

1 ¼ teaspoons kosher salt

4 garlic cloves, chopped

1 pound fresh wild mushrooms, stems removed, sliced

2 cups cherry tomatoes

1 tablespoon fresh thyme leaves

¾ teaspoon black pepper

1 (15-ounce) container ricotta cheese

1 large egg

½ cup water

⅛ teaspoon ground nutmeg

1 bunch fresh basil, torn

4 cups fresh tomato marinara

4 ounces Parmesan cheese, grated (about 1 cup)

1 Preheat the oven to 350°F. Bring a Dutch oven or large saucepan of water to a boil over high. Add the lasagna noodles, and boil until al dente, about 10 minutes. Drain the noodles well, and let cool on a baking sheet.

2 Meanwhile, remove and discard the root ends and dark green tops of the leeks. Cut in half lengthwise, and rinse thoroughly under cold running water to remove grit and sand. Cut into thin strips.

3 Heat 1 ½ tablespoons of the oil in a large skillet over medium. Add the carrots, leeks, and ¼ teaspoon of the salt, and cook, stirring often, until the vegetables just begin to caramelize, about 12 minutes. Stir in the garlic, and cook, stirring often, 3 minutes. Set the mixture aside.

4 Heat 1 tablespoon of the olive oil in a nonstick skillet over high. Add the mushrooms, and cook until seared, about 1 minute. Toss and stir the mushrooms in the skillet until they begin to sweat, 2 to 3 minutes. Add the tomatoes and thyme, and reduce the heat to medium. Sprinkle with ½ teaspoon each of the salt and black pepper, and cook, stirring occasionally, until the tomatoes begin to soften and break down, about 6 minutes.

5 Lightly grease a 12- x 8-inch or 13- x 9-inch baking dish. Stir together the ricotta cheese, egg, ½ cup water, nutmeg, and remaining ½ teaspoon salt and ¼ teaspoon black pepper. Stir in the basil and caramelized leek mixture.

6 Spread 1 tablespoon of the ricotta cheese-and-leek mixture in a thin layer over the bottom of the prepared baking dish. Top with 3 cooked lasagna noodles. Top the noodles with 1½ cups of the mushroom mixture, and spread with 1 ½ cups of the marinara. Top with 1 cup of the ricotta-and-leek mixture. Repeat the layers once, beginning with 3 cooked lasagna noodles and ending with 1 cup of the ricotta-and-leek mixture. Top with the remaining 3 lasagna noodles and 1 cup marinara sauce. Sprinkle the top with the Parmesan, and drizzle with the remaining ½ tablespoon olive oil. Cover the baking dish tightly with aluminum foil.

7 Bake in preheated oven until golden brown, about 45 minutes. Let stand 10 minutes before serving.

SWEET THANG, MAYBE I SHOULDN'T...YEAH, OF COURSE YOU SHOULD

There has always been some way to put the finish to a meal. Centuries ago, "dessert" was dried fruit or candied nuts noshed on after the last course of the meal had been cleared away. Today, we tend to be a little more far-ranging, running the gamut from cakes to cookies to custards to fruit mélanges and sweet-and-savory combinations. I'm partial to the latter—to desserts that balance yin and yang, tangy and cool, savory and sweet—and many of the recipes in this chapter reflect that, but there's plenty here for those who like to bake as well.

And with better alternatives to processed sugar available, there's no reason you can't satisfy sweet cravings heathfully. That means not only should you not think you shouldn't, you absolutely should!

APPLES FOSTER WITH COCONUT-AND-WHISKEY CARAMEL

HANDS-ON: **20 MINUTES**   TOTAL: **20 MINUTES**   SERVES **4** Ⓥ

Did you ever have Bananas Foster? I learned how to make this New Orleans classic when I was 19, tutored by my friend and mentor James Burns. You take butter, brown sugar, rum, and bananas, and basically put 'em together, and the patrons in my friend's restaurant invariably went nuts over it. But when I came to New York and was working as a chef at a restaurant called Black Duck, I made up my own version. And when my mentor's daughter came to New York and dined at Black Duck, she told the owner that my Foster was primo—the best she ever had. That was a pretty proud moment for me, but you be the judge: the recipe is traditional, just decked out with ingredients that are really good for your body—like apples and, of course, whiskey.

- 3 tablespoons unsalted butter
- 6 tablespoons coconut sugar
- 2 tablespoons whiskey
- ¾ cup coconut milk
- 1 teaspoon fresh lemon juice
- ¼ teaspoon ground cinnamon
- 2 firm apples, cut into ¼- to ½-inch-thick rings or wedges (about 2 cups)

Melt the butter in a medium skillet over medium. Whisk in the sugar. Remove the skillet from the heat, and add the whiskey. Carefully ignite the fumes just above the mixture with a long match or long multipurpose lighter. Let the flames die down. Return the skillet to the heat, and add the coconut milk, lemon juice, and cinnamon. Reduce the heat to medium-low, and cook, whisking constantly, until the mixture begins to have the viscosity of caramel, about 4 minutes. Add the apples, and cook, stirring often, until the apples are tender, 8 to 10 minutes. (You'll know the sauce is done when it easily coats the back of a spoon.) Pour this over warm biscuits or some dairy-free ice cream or gelato.

HOW TO FLAMBÉ SAFELY:

Have your equipment and ingredients ready before you start. Use a pan with deep sides and keep the lid handy in case the flames get out of control. Get the pan nice and hot, then move it away from the stove before gently adding your alcohol. (The alcohol you choose should be between 80 to 120 proof.) Use a long match or multipurpose lighter to ignite the alcohol vapors, rather than the liquid directly. Place the pan back on the stove and shake until the flames die down.

PROCESSED SUGAR VS. NATURAL SWEETENERS: WHAT YOU NEED TO KNOW

PROCESSED SUGAR has no place in my home or in my restaurants. All sorts of health-threatening results can kick in when processed sugar is a persistent element in your diet, and in this day and age, when there are so many awesome natural alternatives to sweeten your life, it makes all kinds of sense to leave the processed stuff behind.

I use pretty much any minimally processed or natural sweetener that is not white processed sugar. Each has its own unique flavor and best use. But any added sugar is still sugar so don't go overboard.

DATE SUGAR Made from dried dates. I'm mad about it.

COCONUT SUGAR This tastes a little like brown sugar, but can be high in fructose, so go easy on how much you use.

FRESH FRUIT PUREE

COCONUT NECTAR

MAPLE SYRUP Buy it pure and all natural.

RAW HONEY Honey contains more calories than refined sugar, but because there is nothing sweeter, you don't need as much to satisfy your sweet tooth. Go for raw honey when possible—that is, unpasteurized, unheated, unfiltered, unprocessed in any way—just honey straight from the nectar. That's where the health benefits are, and they are numerous: antibiotic, antiviral, antifungal, and filled with all things good for you.

AGAVE NECTAR There has been a lot of talk around agave. Yes, it is lower on the glycemic index, but it is also way high in fructose. It fits in a vegan diet for sure, but be aware of its downsides, too. If you do use it, make sure it is organic.

Keep in mind that you are cooking or baking to achieve a certain taste, so you'll want to experiment to achieve the profile you're trying to build. You might find, for example, that coconut sugar achieves the right taste but produces a brown color that you didn't want. Or maybe honey is too sweet for a certain dish. Keep going until you find the right alternative for you, knowing that you are in good hands healthwise and living the sweet life.

RICE PUDDING WITH ACORN SQUASH AND CINNAMON

HANDS-ON: **1 HOUR**   TOTAL: **1 HOUR, 10 MINUTES**   SERVES **8**   🄶🄵 Ⓥ

This rice pudding is a warm, creamy, indulgence with the right amount of sweet-flavored cardamom.

1 ⅓ cups uncooked white rice

1 quart plus 1 cup almond milk

4 cups water

½ cup pure maple syrup

2 tablespoons date sugar

3 cardamom pods

1 cinnamon stick

1 star anise pod

½ cup macadamia nuts

3 tablespoons salted butter

½ (1 ½-pound) acorn squash, peeled and cut into ½-inch pieces (about 1 ½ cups)

2 Fuji apples (about 1 ¼ pounds), peeled and cut into ½-inch pieces

2 tablespoons fresh lemon juice (from 1 lemon)

¼ teaspoon kosher salt

1 Process the rice in a blender 20 seconds. Combine the milk and 4 cups water in a large saucepan, and bring to a boil over medium-high. Stir in the rice, syrup, sugar, cardamom pods, cinnamon, and star anise; reduce the heat to low, and simmer, stirring constantly, until creamy, 45 minutes to 1 hour. Remove and discard the cardamom pods, cinnamon, and star anise. Remove from the heat.

2 Preheat the oven to 350°F. Pulse the macadamia nuts in a blender until roughly chopped, 10 to 12 times. Spread the nuts on a parchment paper-lined baking sheet, and bake in preheated oven until fragrant and golden, 8 to 10 minutes.

3 Melt the butter in a large skillet over medium. Add the squash, apples, and lemon juice, and cook, stirring constantly, until tender, about 8 to 10 minutes. Sprinkle with the salt.

4 Spoon the pudding into 8 bowls; top with the squash-apple mixture and macadamia nuts.

FROZEN HONEY MOUSSE WITH LIME AND SEA SALT

HANDS-ON: **30 MINUTES**   TOTAL: **2 HOURS, 30 MINUTES**   SERVES **8**   Ⓥ ⒼⒻ

This summer dessert is as pretty to present as it is delicious. The acidity of the lime smooths out the honey—and honey, we know, cures everything.

3 large pasteurized eggs, separated

¾ cup blossom honey

1 (13.66-ounce) can coconut milk, chilled at least 4 hours

1 cup heavy cream, chilled

1 teaspoon organic vanilla extract

Lime zest

Flaked sea salt (such as Maldon)

1 Whisk together the egg yolks and honey in a medium-size heavy-duty saucepan. Cook over low, whisking constantly, until thickened, 12 to 15 minutes.

2 Beat the egg whites in a medium bowl with an electric mixer fitted with whisk attachment on high until stiff peaks form, 2 to 3 minutes. Set aside.

3 Without shaking or tilting can, carefully open coconut milk. Remove solidified coconut cream from top, and place in a 2-cup measuring cup. Add liquid from can to equal 1 ½ cups, and transfer to a medium bowl. Add heavy cream and vanilla, and beat on medium-high speed until soft peaks form, 2 to 3 minutes. Gently fold the egg whites and honey mixture into the cream mixture; spread in single layer in a 13- x 9-inch glass baking dish. Freeze 2 hours.

4 Spoon into parfait glasses; top with lime zest and sea salt.

FROZEN YUZU-ADE POPS

HANDS-ON: **10 MINUTES**   TOTAL: **6 HOURS, 10 MINUTES**   MAKES **10 POPS**   Ⓥ ⒼⒻ ⒹⒻ

Yuzu is a tart aromatic citrus fruit from Asia that is often used in sauces and seasonings. It's become one of my essential ingredients and it makes these pops both tangy and refreshing.

2 cups boiling water

1 cup bottled yuzu juice

1 cup pineapple juice

1 cup coconut sugar

1 tablespoon raw honey

1 cup cold water

1 Pour the 2 cups boiling water into a large pitcher or mixing bowl. Whisk in the yuzu juice, pineapple juice, sugar, and honey. Add the 1 cup cold water; stir to combine.

2 Pour or ladle the mixture into ice-pop molds or silicon ice cube holders. Add a stick to each mold; freeze for 6 hours.

TIP

You can use almost any combo of fruit juices to make a killer pop. All it takes is fruit juice, sweetener, and a squeeze of lime, if desired. Experiment to find your favorites.

VEGAN CHOCOLATE-FLECKED COCONUT ICE CREAM

HANDS-ON: **20 MINUTES**   TOTAL: **9 HOURS, 40 MINUTES**   SERVES **8**   VG GF DF

With all the great plant-based milks now widely available, dairy-free ice cream is now easily made at home. Whether you do dairy or not, this luscious, dreamy treat is sure to make anyone savor every spoonful.

2 (13.66-ounce) cans coconut milk

½ cup pure maple syrup

1 tablespoon arrowroot starch

¼ teaspoon fine sea salt

1 ½ teaspoons vanilla extract

¼ teaspoon almond extract

1 (4-ounce) bittersweet chocolate baking bar

1 Whisk together the coconut milk, syrup, arrowroot starch, and salt in a medium saucepan. Cook over medium, stirring constantly, until the mixture thickens slightly and coats the back of a spoon, 6 to 8 minutes. (Do not boil.) Remove from the heat; stir in the extracts, and cool completely, about 1 hour. Transfer to a bowl; cover and chill until very cold, at least 4 hours.

2 Grate the bittersweet chocolate on the medium holes of a box grater. Pour the chilled mixture into the frozen freezer bowl of a 1 ½-quart electric ice-cream maker, and proceed according to the manufacturer's directions , adding the chocolate to the ice-cream mixture during the last 2 minutes. (Directions and time may vary.) Transfer the ice cream to a freezer-safe container; cover and freeze until firm, about 4 hours.

CAPPUCCINO CASHEW ICE CREAM

HANDS-ON: **10 MINUTES**   TOTAL: **8 HOURS, 30 MINUTES**   SERVES **8**   VG GF DF

This cashew ice cream is as rich and creamy as traditional ice cream but without the dairy, eggs, or any refined sugar. Try unsweetened almond milk instead of cashew milk, if you prefer.

¾ cup raw unsalted cashews

2 cups water

¾ cup warm strong-brewed coffee

¼ cup coconut oil, at room temperature (solid)

1 cup pure maple syrup

1 cup unsweetened cashew milk

¼ cup peanut oil

1 teaspoon vanilla extract

½ teaspoon fine sea salt

1 Soak the cashews in the 2 cups water at room temperature at least 8 hours; drain.

2 Process the cashews, coffee, and coconut oil in a blender until smooth. Add the maple syrup, cashew milk, peanut oil, vanilla, and salt; process until smooth. Cover and refrigerate 4 hours or until well chilled.

3 Pour the mixture into the frozen freezer bowl of a 1 ½-quart electric ice-cream maker, and proceed according to the manufacturer's directions. (Directions and times may vary.) Transfer to an airtight freezer-safe container; freeze until firm, about 4 hours.

COCONUT CARAMEL SAUCE

HANDS-ON: **25 MINUTES**   TOTAL: **55 MINUTES**   SERVES **10**   VG GF DF

This smooth, decadent dairy-free sauce is amazing with the ice cream or Dark Chocolate Soufflés (page 220).

1 (13.66-ounce) can coconut milk

⅔ cup coconut sugar

¼ teaspoon fine sea salt

1 teaspoon vanilla extract

1 Combine the coconut milk, coconut sugar, and salt in a medium saucepan; bring to a boil over medium, stirring occasionally. Reduce the heat to low, and simmer, stirring occasionally, until the mixture is thick and deep amber in color, 20 to 25 minutes.

2 Remove from the heat, and stir in the vanilla. Cool the mixture completely, about 30 minutes, stirring occasionally. Serve immediately, or refrigerate the mixture in an airtight container up to 1 week.

CINNAMON-NUTMEG GLUTEN-FREE CHURROS

HANDS-ON: **45 MINUTES**   TOTAL: **45 MINUTES**   SERVES **12 TO 16**   Ⓥ ⒼⒻ

Churros, originally a Spanish classic, are now just about everywhere thankfully, because this fried-dough pastry tastes like a gift from the gods. These cinnamon-nutmeg churros encompass all the flavors of the original, but are gluten-free.

6 cups safflower oil

1 cup water

4 ounces (½ cup) unsalted butter

¼ teaspoon kosher salt

⅝ cup plus 1 tablespoon coconut sugar

1 cup (about 4 ¼ ounces) gluten-free flour

½ teaspoon xanthan gum

3 large eggs, at room temperature

1 teaspoon ground cinnamon

½ teaspoon ground nutmeg

Lime zest, optional

1 Heat the oil in a large Dutch oven over medium to 350°F. (The length of the churros is about 6 inches, so the Dutch oven should be large enough to accommodate that length.)

2 Meanwhile, combine the 1 cup water and butter in a medium saucepan. Bring to a boil over medium-high; boil, whisking constantly, until the butter is melted, about 1 minute. Add the salt and 1 tablespoon of the coconut sugar; return to a boil. Add the gluten-free flour and xanthan gum, and cook, stirring constantly, until the mixture forms a slightly sticky dough, 1 to 1 ½ minutes. Remove from the heat immediately. (Be careful not to overcook.)

3 Transfer the dough to the bowl of a heavy-duty stand mixer. Add the eggs, 1 at a time, and beat at high speed until incorporated after each addition. Continue to beat at high speed until the dough becomes shiny and smooth, 2 to 3 minutes. Let the dough stand 10 to 15 minutes.

4 Stir together the cinnamon, nutmeg, and remaining ⅝ cup coconut sugar in a rectangular baking pan or dish.

5 Insert metal tip no. 843 or a ½-inch closed star tip into a pastry bag. Fill the pastry bag with the churro dough, and pipe a 4- to 6-inch length into the hot oil; fry the churro until the underside begins to turn golden, about 2 minutes. (Adjust the heat as necessary to maintain the oil temperature at 350°F.) Using a heatproof spoon or spatula, turn the churro, and fry until golden brown, 2 to 3 more minutes. Drain on paper towels until cool enough to handle, about 1 minute. Carefully dredge the churro in the cinnamon-sugar mixture. Repeat with the remaining dough.

6 Serve warm; garnish with the lime zest, if desired.

VEGAN CHOCOLATE CHIP AND SALTED CHILI COOKIES

HANDS-ON: **25 MINUTES**   TOTAL: **50 MINUTES**   MAKES **3 DOZEN COOKIES**   (VG)

At my restaurant Pretty Southern, I offer classic comforts that people already know and love, but I update the recipes so everyone can enjoy them. These scrumptious cookies put sweet and savory together in the best way.

- 2 cups (about 8.5 ounces) organic flour
- 1 ¼ teaspoon baking soda
- 1 ½ teaspoon smoked ancho chili powder
- 1 ½ teaspoon fine sea salt, plus more to finish
- 1 ¾ cup coconut sugar
- ¼ cup date sugar
- ½ cup coconut oil
- ¼ cup organic apple cider
- 2 tablespoons applesauce or apple puree
- 1 to 2 tablespoons almond milk or water, if needed
- 1 ¾ cups dark chocolate chips (70% cacao)

1 Preheat the oven to 350°F. Line 2 baking sheets with parchment paper.

2 Whisk together the flour, baking soda, chili powder, and salt in a bowl.

3 Combine the coconut and date sugars, coconut oil, cider, and applesauce in a bowl. Beat with an electric mixer at medium-high speed until well blended. Gradually add the flour mixture, beating at low speed just until blended. (If the dough looks dry, beat in 1 to 2 tablespoons almond milk or water, a little at a time, just until the dough comes together.) Stir in the chocolate chips.

4 Drop the dough by rounded spoonfuls onto the prepared baking sheets, 2 inches apart.

5 Sprinkle the dough with the sea salt.

6 Bake in preheated oven, in batches, until the edges are set, 10 to 12 minutes. Cool the cookies on wire racks.

DARK CHOCOLATE SOUFFLÉS
WITH RUM CREAM

HANDS-ON: **20 MINUTES**   TOTAL: **40 MINUTES**   SERVES **6**   Ⓥ ⒼⒻ

Light and airy yet rich and chocolaty, this soufflé is ready to impress.

1 (13.66-ounce) can coconut milk, chilled at least 4 hours

1 ½ tablespoons pure maple syrup

1 ½ tablespoons dark rum

1 tablespoon coconut oil, at room temperature (solid)

1 tablespoon unsweetened cocoa

2 (4-ounce) bittersweet chocolate baking bars, chopped

3 large egg yolks

⅛ teaspoon fine sea salt

½ cup coconut sugar

4 large egg whites

Coconut Caramel Sauce (page 215), optional

1 Place a bowl and electric mixer beaters in the freezer for 15 minutes. Without shaking or tilting the can, carefully open the coconut milk, and remove the solidified coconut cream from the top; place in the chilled bowl. (Reserve the coconut water in the bottom of the can for another use.) Add the maple syrup and rum to the coconut cream, and beat with the cold beaters of an electric mixer at high speed until stiff peaks form. Cover and chill until ready to serve.

2 Preheat the oven to 400°F. Grease 6 (6-ounce) ramekins with the coconut oil; sprinkle with the unsweetened cocoa. Place the ramekins on a baking sheet.

3 Microwave the bittersweet chocolate in a small microwave-safe bowl at HIGH until melted, 1 to 1 ½ minutes, stirring every 30 seconds. Beat the egg yolks, salt, and ¼ cup of the coconut sugar with an electric mixer at high speed until thick and pale, about 4 minutes. Gradually fold in the melted chocolate.

4 Beat the egg whites with an electric mixer at high speed until foamy; gradually add the remaining ¼ cup coconut sugar, 1 tablespoon at a time, beating until soft peaks form. Fold one-third of the egg white mixture into the chocolate mixture until well combined; gently fold in the remaining egg white mixture just until blended. Divide the batter among the prepared ramekins.

5 Bake in preheated oven until puffed above rim and set, 15 to 20 minutes. Serve immediately with the whipped coconut cream mixture and, if desired, Coconut Caramel Sauce.

WARM BERRY COMPOTE

HANDS-ON: **8 MINUTES**   TOTAL: **8 MINUTES**   SERVES **4** Ⓥ ⒼⒻ

Berries are packed with fiber, antioxidants, and vitamins. But all you need to know is that this berry compote can also dress up everything from ice cream to French toast and waffles.

1 teaspoon butter

2 tablespoons raw honey

2 teaspoons fresh lemon juice

Dash of ground cinnamon

2 cups fresh mixed berries

Melt the butter in a saucepan over medium. Add the honey, lemon juice, dash of ground cinnamon, and mixed berries; bring to a boil. Reduce the heat; simmer 5 minutes.

TIP

This recipe makes 1 ⅓ cups. Store in an airtight container in the fridge for up to 1 week.

BLACKBERRY SHORTCAKES WITH ALMOND CREAM

HANDS-ON: **20 MINUTES** TOTAL: **40 MINUTES** SERVES **8** (V)

A healthy treat that relies on the berries and almond milk cream for sweetness. Use a mix of strawberries, raspberries, or blueberries to add more color.

- ½ cup grapeseed oil
- ½ teaspoon vanilla extract
- ½ teaspoon xanthan gum
- 1 ¼ cups plus 1 tablespoon cold unsweetened almond milk
- 3 tablespoons raw honey
- 2 tablespoons amaretto liqueur
- 2 cups fresh blackberries
- 2 cups (about 7 ounces) whole-wheat pastry flour, plus more for kneading
- 1 tablespoon baking powder
- ½ teaspoon fine sea salt
- 2 ounces (¼ cup) cold unsalted butter, cubed
- 3 tablespoons sliced almonds

1 Process the oil, vanilla, xanthan gum, ½ cup of the almond milk, 1 tablespoon of the honey, and 1 tablespoon of the amaretto in a blender or food processor until soft peaks form, 1 to 2 minutes. Transfer to a bowl; cover and chill 2 hours and up to 1 week.

2 Combine the blackberries and remaining 1 tablespoon amaretto and 2 tablespoons honey in a large bowl, and toss to coat. Let stand at room temperature 30 minutes.

3 Preheat the oven to 425°F. Line a cookie sheet with parchment paper. Stir together the flour, baking powder, and salt in a medium bowl. Cut in the butter using a pastry blender until the mixture resembles small peas. Add ¾ cup of the almond milk, stirring just until combined.

4 Turn the dough out onto a lightly floured surface; knead 3 or 4 times. Roll or pat the dough to ¾-inch thickness. Cut with a 2 ½-inch round biscuit cutter to make 8 shortcakes, and place 1 inch apart on the prepared baking sheet. Brush the tops with the remaining 1 tablespoon almond milk, and sprinkle with the sliced almonds. Bake in preheated oven until lightly browned, 10 to 12 minutes. Transfer the cookie sheet to a wire rack, and cool the shortcakes completely, about 30 minutes.

5 Split the shortcakes. Spoon the blackberry mixture onto the bottom of the shortcakes; dollop with the cold almond cream, and cover with the shortcake tops.

GLUTEN-FREE BERRY ESPRESSO BUCKLE

HANDS-ON: 25 MINUTES TOTAL: **1 HOUR** SERVES **8** Ⓥ ⒼⒻ

Have you heard of coffee cake? This puts it to shame.

CAKE

¼ cup coconut oil, plus more for preparing the pan

1 cup organic coconut sugar

1 large egg

1 cup coconut milk

2 cups gluten-free flour

2 teaspoons baking powder

2 cups fresh berries (a mix of blueberries, raspberries, or blackberries)

STREUSEL

⅓ cup organic brown sugar

⅓ cup (about 1.5 ounces) gluten-free flour

½ teaspoon instant espresso powder

½ teaspoon ground cinnamon

2 ounces (¼ cup) unsalted butter, cubed

ICING

½ cup organic coconut palm sugar, blended in a high-power blender to a fine powder

1 tablespoon lemon juice

1 tablespoon water

¼ teaspoon vanilla extract

1 Preheat the oven to 375°F. Grease a 9-inch round cake pan with a bit of coconut oil.

2 To prepare the Cake: beat the ¼ cup coconut oil and coconut sugar with an electric mixer at medium speed until combined. Add the egg, beating until blended. Add the milk; beat until just blended.

3 Whisk together the 2 cups gluten-free flour and baking powder in a medium bowl; gradually add to the coconut oil mixture, beating at low speed until just combined. Gently fold in the berries. Spoon the batter into the prepared pan.

4 To prepare the Streusel: combine the brown sugar, ⅓ cup flour, espresso, and cinnamon in a small bowl. Work in the butter using your fingertips or a fork to combine. Continue until the mixture is crumbly. Sprinkle on top of the batter. Bake in preheated oven 35 to 40 minutes, or until the top is golden and a wooden pick inserted in the center comes out clean. Cool the cake in the pan on a wire rack for 15 minutes before removing it from the pan and placing it, streusel side up, on a serving plate.

5 To prepare the Icing: while the cake is cooling, combine the powdered palm sugar, lemon juice, 1 tablespoon water, and vanilla. Drizzle on the buckle before slicing and serving.

BLACK SESAME-PEACH CAKES

HANDS-ON: **15 MINUTES** TOTAL: **45 MINUTES** SERVES **16** (V) (GF)

I've turned the classic applesauce cake into a peachsauce cake. The result is moist, lower in sugar and carbohydrates than any cake out there, and perfectly delicious. Serve with whipped cream, ice cream, fruit, or anything else that strikes your fancy!

1 (16-ounce) package frozen sliced peaches, thawed

4 ounces (½ cup) unsalted butter, softened, plus more for greasing pans

1 cup date sugar

2 tablespoons raw honey

2 cups (about 8.5 ounces) gluten-free baking flour, plus more for flouring pans

2 teaspoons baking soda

1 teaspoon kosher salt

1 teaspoon ground cinnamon

¼ teaspoon Chinese five-spice powder

2 large eggs

1 cup chopped dried peaches, soaked in ice-cold water for 1 hour, drained

¼ cup toasted black sesame seeds

1 tablespoon olive oil

1 vanilla bean

Lime zest for garnish, optional

1 Preheat the oven to 350°F. Butter and lightly flour 2 (8-inch) round cake pans. Process the thawed peach slices in a food processor until smooth, about 1 minute; set aside.

2 Beat the 4 ounces butter, sugar, and honey with an electric mixer at medium speed until well blended. Stir together the 2 cups flour, baking soda, salt, cinnamon, and five-spice powder in a medium bowl.

3 Add the eggs, pureed peaches, and flour mixture to the butter mixture, and beat until just incorporated. Stir in the dried peaches, sesame seeds, and olive oil. Split the vanilla bean, and scrape the seeds into the mixture; stir until incorporated. Reserve the vanilla bean pod for another use.

4 Pour the batter into the prepared pans, and bake in preheated oven until a wooden pick inserted in the center comes out clean, 25 to 35 minutes. Cool the cakes in pans on wire racks 5 minutes. Remove from the pans, and cut each cake into 8 wedges. Garnish with the lime zest.

BASIC RECIPES

HOMEMADE ALMOND BUTTER

HANDS-ON: **5 MINUTES** TOTAL: **5 MINUTES** SERVES **16** GF V DF

Nut butters like almond butter are a good source of protein and healthy fat. Make your own to eliminate excess salt, sugar, and oils.

2 cups roasted whole almonds or slivered roasted almonds

1 ¼ teaspoon raw honey

½ to 1 teaspoon kosher salt

Place the nuts, honey, and salt in a food processor, and process until they form a paste, about 2 ½ minutes for whole roasted almonds, 3 ½ minutes for slivered roasted almonds.

HOMEMADE CASHEW BUTTER

HANDS-ON: **5 MINUTES** TOTAL: **5 MINUTES** SERVES **16** GF V DF

This smooth butter can be used as a substitute for tahini.

2 cups raw cashews

1 ¼ teaspoon raw honey

½ to 1 teaspoon kosher salt

Place the nuts, honey, and salt in a food processor, and process until they form a paste, about 2 minutes.

100% REAL

HOMEMADE PEANUT BUTTER

HANDS-ON: **5 MINUTES**   TOTAL: **5 MINUTES**   SERVES **16**   GF V DF

Use plain roasted peanuts instead of dry-roasted, which are seasoned with paprika, onion, and garlic powders.

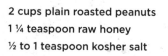

2 cups plain roasted peanuts

1 ¼ teaspoon raw honey

½ to 1 teaspoon kosher salt

Place the nuts, honey, and salt in a food processor, and process until they form a paste, about 2 minutes.

HOMEMADE WALNUT BUTTER

HANDS-ON: **5 MINUTES**   TOTAL: **5 MINUTES**   SERVES **16**   GF V DF

Walnuts are high in antioxidants and contain omega-3 fatty acids, but they are also high in saturated fat so take it easy when using.

2 cups roasted or raw walnut pieces

1 ¼ teaspoon raw honey

½ to 1 teaspoon kosher salt

Place the nuts, honey, and salt in a food processor, and process until they form a paste, about 1 minute.

CHILI VINEGAR

HANDS-ON: **10 MINUTES**   TOTAL: **10 MINUTES**   MAKES **2 CUPS**   GF DF VG

This elevates and brightens a dish with acid, salt, and a little heat. I use it on everything. You can keep it in an airtight container for several months.

20 dried chiles, each 2 inches long

4 red Fresno chiles

4 jalapeño chiles

4 cloves of garlic, smashed

3 parsley sprigs

4 cilantro leaves

2 shallots, shaved paper thin on mandoline

2 cups white wine vinegar

Combine all the ingredients in a saucepan over medium-high. Bring to a boil. Cool down to room temperature and use.

TOMATO SOFRITO

HANDS-ON: **10 MINUTES**   TOTAL: **10 MINUTES, PLUS CHILLING**   MAKES **3 CUPS**   GF DF VG

Is it a sauce, vinaigrette, or accompaniment? It's all three—or just about anything else you can think of. Every culture has its own version of sofrito—from Thailand to Italy, from western Africa to the Caribbean, from Spain to Puerto Rico. Here is my version. At the end, you might also like to add one or two tablespoons of fruity olive oil.

2 tablespoons olive oil

3 large ripe tomatoes, quartered, seeds removed

1 shallot, finely chopped

1 tablespoon finely chopped serrano chile, seeds removed

2 garlic cloves, finely chopped

2 tablespoons fresh lemon juice

⅓ cup thinly sliced fresh cilantro

2 teaspoons fine sea salt

½ teaspoon black pepper

Heat oil in a large skillet over medium. Add tomatoes, shallot, chile, and garlic. Cook, stirring often, 5 minutes. Remove from heat, and stir in lemon juice. Transfer to a blender or food processor; process until smooth. Transfer to a bowl, and chill until cool, 15 to 20 minutes. Stir in cilantro, salt, and pepper.

TIP

To store, pour the sofrito into ice cube trays and keep the frozen cubes in a zip-top freezer bag to use as needed.

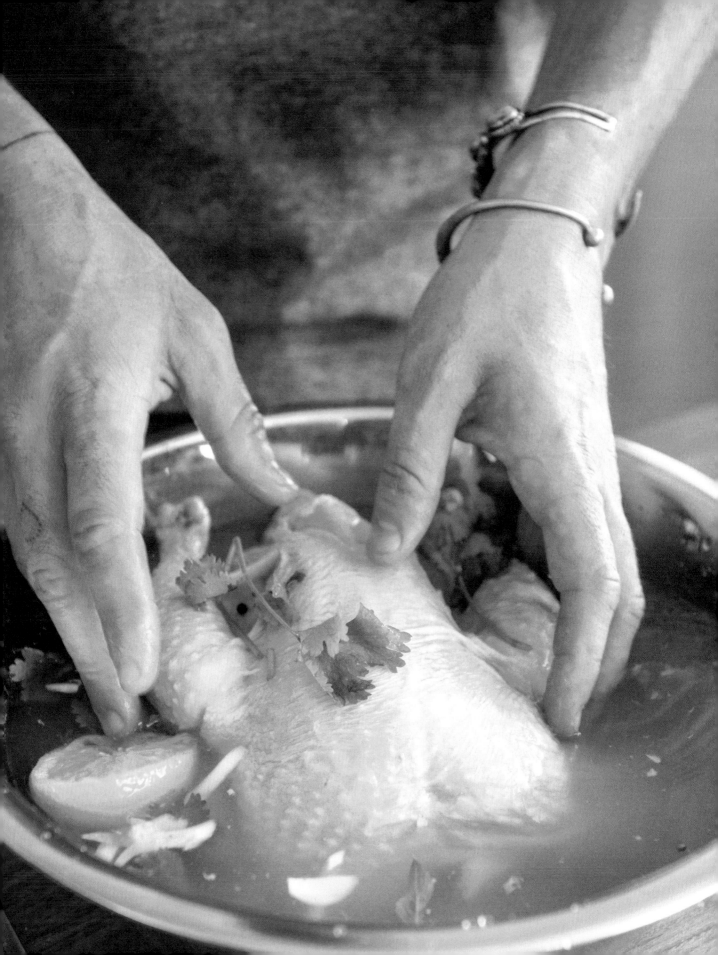

CHICKEN BRINE

HANDS-ON: **10 MINUTES** TOTAL: **3 HOURS, 10 MINUTES** MAKES **ENOUGH FOR A 4-POUND CHICKEN**

Brining isn't just for your Thanksgiving turkey. Use it anytime you roast or fry chicken to ensure it stays juicy.

15 ounces (about 2 cups) of water

⅓ cup (3 ounces) of salt

2 tablespoons Tamari sauce

Fresh herbs, such as cilantro, rosemary, and thyme

3 garlic cloves

1 one-inch piece of ginger, smashed

1 small onion, sliced

1 lemon, halved

2 teaspoons black peppercorns, freshly cracked

4 cups of ice

Combine all ingredients except the ice in a large pot on high. Once the mixture comes to a boil, turn off the heat and add the ice to chill the mixture. Then add a whole chicken; the brine will suffice for a chicken of about 3 to 4 pounds in weight. Soak for at least 3 hours.

Juicy raspberries are antioxidant-rich brain boosters.

METRIC EQUIVALENTS

The information in the following chart is provided to help cooks outside the United States successfully use the recipes in this book. All equivalents are approximate.

COOKING/OVEN TEMPERATURES

	Fahrenheit	Celsius	Gas Mark
Freeze Water	32° F	0° C	
Room Temp.	68° F	20° C	
Boil Water	212° F	100° C	
Bake	325° F	160° C	3
	350° F	180° C	4
	375° F	190° C	5
	400° F	200° C	6
	425° F	220° C	7
	450° F	230° C	8
Broil			Grill

LIQUID INGREDIENTS BY VOLUME

$\frac{1}{4}$ tsp	=					1 ml
$\frac{1}{2}$ tsp	=					2 ml
1 tsp	=					5 ml
3 tsp	=	1 Tbsp	=	$\frac{1}{2}$ fl oz	=	15 ml
2 Tbsp	=	$\frac{1}{8}$ cup	=	1 fl oz	=	30 ml
4 Tbsp	=	$\frac{1}{4}$ cup	=	2 fl oz	=	60 ml
$5\frac{1}{3}$ Tbsp	=	$\frac{1}{3}$ cup	=	3 fl oz	=	80 ml
8 Tbsp	=	$\frac{1}{2}$ cup	=	4 fl oz	=	120 ml
$10\frac{2}{3}$ Tbsp	=	$\frac{2}{3}$ cup	=	5 fl oz	=	160 ml
12 Tbsp	=	$\frac{3}{4}$ cup	=	6 fl oz	=	180 ml
16 Tbsp	=	1 cup	=	8 fl oz	=	240 ml
1 pt	=	2 cups	=	16 fl oz	=	480 ml
1 qt	=	4 cups	=	32 fl oz	=	960 ml
				33 fl oz	=	1000 ml = 1 l

(To convert ounces to grams, multiply the number of ounces by 30.)

1 oz	=	$\frac{1}{16}$ lb	=	30 g
4 oz	=	$\frac{1}{4}$ lb	=	120 g
8 oz	=	$\frac{1}{2}$ lb	=	240 g
12 oz	=	$\frac{3}{4}$ lb	=	360 g
16 oz	=	1 lb	=	480 g

EQUIVALENTS FOR DIFFERENT TYPES OF INGREDIENTS

Standard Cup	Fine Powder* (ex. flour)	Grain (ex. rice)	Granular (ex. sugar)	Liquid Solids (ex. butter)	Liquid (ex. milk)
1	120 g	150 g	190 g	200 g	240 ml
$\frac{3}{4}$	90 g	113 g	143 g	150 g	180 ml
$\frac{2}{3}$	80 g	100 g	125 g	133 g	160 ml
$\frac{1}{2}$	60 g	75 g	95 g	100 g	120 ml
$\frac{1}{3}$	40 g	50 g	63 g	67 g	80 ml
$\frac{1}{4}$	30 g	38 g	48 g	50 g	60 ml
$\frac{1}{8}$	15 g	19 g	24 g	25 g	30 ml

* Metrics based on King Arthur Flour.

LENGTH

(To convert inches to centimeters, multiply the number of inches by 2.5.)

1 in	=					2.5 cm
6 in	=	$\frac{1}{2}$ ft			=	15 cm
12 in	=	1 ft			=	30 cm
36 in	=	3 ft	=	1 yd	=	90 cm
40 in	=					100 cm = 1 m

ACKNOWLEDGMENTS

For their assistance in making *100% Real* become a reality, I couldn't be more thankful to the following people.

Susanna Margolis for navigating, guiding, and helping me get my thoughts on paper. You are a star. A bright one!

Betty Wong and the team at Time Inc. Books, including designer Allison Chi, thank you so much! This couldn't have been possible without your persistence and dedication.

My lawyer, literary agent, and friend Geoff Menin. Thank you, my friend.

My manager, Joel Menzin, you are a constant reminder to always keep my head high no matter what. (Sh*t! This whole damn time I thought you meant the other kind.) I appreciate you daily, my man.

Evan Sung, you take beautiful photos, bravo! Thank you.

And lastly, my mom, Diane, who has stuck by my side through epic times and really gnarly ones. I aim to parent like you one day soon. . .

Did you know? 1 in 11 people have some form of diabetes.

EDUCATE, ADVOCATE AND CURE.

BEY⚬ND TYPE 1

In 2015, I got together with singer-actor Nick Jonas and two remarkable mothers of kids diagnosed with type 1 diabetes, Juliette de Baubigny and Sarah Lucas, and we formed an organization called Beyond Type 1. Part support group, part social community, part campaign for a cure, BT1 above all advocates for programs, technologies, and innovations that help those of us diagnosed with type 1 diabetes thrive in every way.

Through special events, fundraising, and educational outreach, we strive to make a simple point: Diabetes is a chronic disease; it's not a definition of who we are. We can and do live rich, full lives well beyond the diagnosis of our disease.

Precisely because eating is something we all have to do, pretty much three times a day, the kitchen is a key place where we can advance the richness and fullness of our lives—in ways that make the best sense for our bodies. Approach food with love and creativity and a commitment to the body's health and longevity, as the recipes in this book do, and whatever "diagnosis" you carry, you'll be enriching yourself, boosting your strength, and taking pleasure in every bite.

To learn more, please check out beyondtype1.org.

RESOURCES

SPECIALTY INGREDIENTS

You don't need to prowl out-of-the-way health food stores to find the ingredients used in this book. Get them at your local Albertsons, Publix, Safeway, Sprouts, Target, Trader Joe's, Walgreens, Walmart, Winn-Dixie, and Whole Foods or online at some of these retailers.

ANSON MILLS
www.ansonmills.com
Based in my old stomping grounds in South Carolina, they grow and mill heritage and heirloom grains. I think these are the best grits in the U.S.

KALUSTYAN'S
www.kalustyans.com
New York City's specialty food playground

RANCHO GORDO
www.ranchogordo.com
For beans, spices, and more

ZINGERMAN'S
www.zingermans.com
An amazing place for foodie gifts and kits

KITCHEN EQUIPMENT

KORIN
www.korin.com
For a sharp, reliable western-style knife

THE BROOKLYN KITCHEN
www.thebrooklynkitchen.com
For equipment and ingredients

FARMERS' MARKETS

GROWNYC
www.grownyc.org
Organizes NYC's network of farmers' markets and community gardens, including Union Square Greenmarket and Brooklyn's McCarren Park Greenmarket

U.S. DEPARTMENT OF AGRICULTURE
www.ams.usda.gov/local-food-directories/farmersmarkets
Find a local farmers' market using this national directory.

ENVIRONMENTAL RESOURCES

THE MONTEREY BAY AQUARIUM'S SEAFOOD WATCH
www.seafoodwatch.org
For information on sustainable seafood

SUPERMOMS AGAINST SUPERBUGS
www.saveantibiotics.org
Advocates for regulating the use of antibiotics on farms and food animals

INDEX

SAM TALBOT is a chef, author, philanthropist, and television personality. Diagnosed at a young age with type 1 diabetes, he has a deep understanding of the impact of food on life. This unique perspective has become the driving force in all of his projects and has put him at the forefront of the sustainable living movement. He was the founding Executive Chef of The Surf Lodge in Montauk, NY, and went on to open Imperial No. Nine at the Mondrian SoHo. He is the chef and owner of Pretty Southern in Brooklyn, and the co-founder of Beyond Type 1, a nonprofit organization focusing on the diabetes community.